Yellowstone
WOLVES

In the Wild

Yellowstone
WOLVES
In the Wild

BY JAMES C. HALFPENNY, PHD

FOREWORD BY DOUGLAS W. SMITH, PHD

YELLOWSTONE WOLF PROJECT LEADER

Published by Riverbend Publishing, Helena, Montana

Cover design by Jeff Wincapaw
Text design by DD Dowden

Printed in South Korea
1 2 3 4 5 6 7 8 9 0 SI 10 09 08 07 06 05 04 03

Yellowstone Wolves in the Wild
ISBN 1-931832-26-9
Cataloging-in-Publication data is on file at the Library of Congress.

RIVERBEND PUBLISHING
P.O. Box 5833
Helena, MT 59604
1-866-787-2363 (toll-free)
www.riverbendpublishing.com

DEDICATION

*To Elaine Anderson, for the miles we walked,
the bears and wolves we watched,
the stories we shared, the laughs we laughed,
and the joy that you brought to us.
I love you!*

PHOTO CREDITS
FRONT COVER: Donald M. Jones
BACK COVER: five wolves on hillside, Dan Hartman;
                swimming wolf and wolf in trees, Jess R. Lee;
                standing wolf, Donald M. Jones
TITLE PAGE: Donald M. Jones

ACKNOWLEDGMENTS

This book grew from the hearts of the wolf watchers, especially those along the road in Lamar Valley. It is a product of the questions asked by my students and the answers found by all who have watched wolves. It would not have happened without the generosity of sharing by watchers, researchers, field companions, and most importantly friends.

Forming the backbone of this book is the knowledge gained by the Yellowstone Wolf Research Project for without that foundation the book would have never happened. My sincere thanks to Mike Phillips, Doug Smith, Deb Guernsey, Kerry Murphy, and Dan Stahler. To each of the volunteers who helped, especially for their long cold hours, I also give special thanks. If the reader sees a fact in this book, somehow it is related to or derived from the efforts of personnel at the Yellowstone Wolf Research Project. It is important to note that in this book one biologist may report ideas or findings that are, in fact, the result of many researchers collaborating with the Wolf Project. I thank everyone who has contributed to the historical development of ideas, concepts, and research and I apologize if some names cannot be included in the abbreviated coverage of these topics.

Many have helped to increase our knowledge of the wolf and many have shared their stories with me. This book is a tribute to the generous input of: Elaine Anderson, Val Asher, Ed Bangs, Norm Bishop, Christine Blackmor, Valerie Blackmor, Cliff Brown, Pam (Gontz) Cahill, Marc Catellier, Chris Cauble, Hank Fisher, Jim Garry, Deb Guernsey, Dan and Cindy Hartman, Ward Hughson, Mike Jimenez, Mark Johnson, Minnette Johnson, Wayne Kendal, Bob Landis, Deb Lineweaver, Rick McIntyre, Dan MacNulty, David Mech, Jeanne Muellner, Kerry Murphy, Rolf Peterson, Maggie Purves, Janet Ross, Toni Ruth, Jennifer Sands, Doug Smith, Dan Stahler, Dan Tyers, Linda Thurston, John Varley, Nathan Varley, Gerlie Weinstein, Bill Wengler, Anne Whitbeck, and Jason Wilson.

Others, including Renee Askins, Wayne Brewster, Bob Crabtree, Hank Fisher, Pat Tucker, Bruce Weide, and Alice Whitlaw provided help over the longer run and are equally appreciated.

Special thanks to Marc Catellier for his efforts to make the book a success. Let me also thank those who, due to the frailty of my mind, I may have inadvertently failed to acknowledge.

Most importantly, my heartfelt thank you to my alpha partner, Diann Thompson, for your love and encouragement.

To my friends, I say, long may the winds blows, the snows fall, and wolves howl. Let's keep Yellowstone wild!

A black wolf trots through fresh snow and sagebrush in Yellowstone National Park. About 46 percent of Yellowstone's wolves are black, an unusually high percentage. Most wolves in North America are gray. Of the 31 Canadian wolves released into Yellowstone in 1995 and 1996, 12 were black or dark furred. MICHAEL H. FRANCIS.

CONTENTS

A yearling wolf of the Druid Peak pack stands alert after feeding on an elk carcass. The "Druids" are Yellowstone's most watched wolves. The pack inhabits the Lamar Valley and pack members are frequently seen from the park road. DONALD M. JONES

FOREWORD

A longstanding goal and ideal for park management is to return our protected areas to their most primeval, natural state. There has been considerable debate (often times unproductive) over what constitutes natural, but wolves are not part of this debate. Without question wolves are the essence of wild nature or, if you choose other words, the fundamental aspect to what is natural. It is well known what our landscapes are like without the wolf, so well known it turned some of our greatest biological minds—Aldo Leopold, Adolph Murie, Sigurd Olson—toward wolves as a subject of study and as a defining feature to what was wild nature. So Yellowstone, the mother park, wolf-less since 1926, and despite its other world-renowned accolades, was without the beating heart of wildness. But through nothing short of near miraculous, tireless efforts, wolves were reintroduced to Yellowstone in 1995 and 1996.

Now, eight years later, wildness is restored. Although this may seem like the end to a battle lasting more than 20 years, it is not the end. What eliminated the wolf seven decades ago—fear, misunderstanding, hatred—still persist. Propaganda and misinformation still plague wolf management and make wolves among the most controversial of all wildlife species. Their notoriety makes them prominent in people's minds, but many people do not know the real wolf. Wolf opponents, because their message is simple and allied with folklore, reach great numbers of people who hear nothing else. Accurate information about wolves may be the most pressing issue for wolf managers.

Yellowstone Wolves in the Wild by Jim Halfpenny makes significant progress toward advancing a true representation of what wolves are really like. Jim tells the true tales, chronicling how this top carnivore became established in the world's first national park after a decades-long absence. Many of the stories are related through the words of the people doing the research, others through the people who watch wolves throughout the year or for weeks at a time. This tremendous dedication has revealed wolves in ways never before documented. The book pays homage to these people, affectionately called "wolf watchers," rightfully giving them credit for information they contribute to our understanding of wolves in the wild.

This watching underscores the amazing and unpredicted visibility of wolves in Yellowstone. Wolves are visible somewhere in the park virtually every day. In June 2002, the 100,000 visitor laid her eyes on a wolf—a phenomenal statistic. I worked on wolves for 13 years in Isle Royale National Park, hiking 500 miles each summer, and if I saw one wolf it was an accomplishment. Typically my Isle Royale sighting was under one minute, and now in Yellowstone "wolf watchers" observe wolves in all kinds of behavior no one ever thought was possible. We were unprepared for this kind of experience and had to revise our research plans to capture this unusual aspect of Yellowstone wolves. It is here that "wolf watchers" have really paid off, for every day that wolves are visible, there is somebody waiting to watch them. Almost always they faithfully report their observations, helping us advance our understanding of this much maligned carnivore who still—unbelievably and despite being one of the most well studied mammals—has a public relations problem.

This book is therefore as much a tribute to all these people who have contributed to our understanding of wolves as it is a tribute to the wolves themselves. This book will be most valuable to the people on the roads in Yellowstone watching wolves. But do not let the value of the book end there. Know there are people listening to your stories, people like Jim Halfpenny, who are taking the time to compile these stories, write them down, and tell the real tales. These are not fairy tales based on myths from the turn of the century but the factual stories behind Yellowstone's new wolves. In the end, of course, none of these stories about wolves are "new." Wolves were here and should never have been exterminated. Yellowstone as the first national park came too early for many to know the value of a wolf, the value wolves confer on an ecosystem and on the idea of wildness—something more often lost than gained in our modern world. Park policy calls it natural. I call it about time that the top carnivore is back in one of the last great wildlands in the continental United States.

Douglas W. Smith, Yellowstone Wolf Project Leader
Yellowstone National Park, Wyoming

The alpha female of the Druid Peak pack, 42F, howls for the rest of her pack. Yellowstone visitors see wolves more often than they actually hear wolves. Hearing a wolf howl requires patience and quiet watching. MARK MILLER

PREFACE

TO SEE A WOLF

Students from my wolf class and I watched spellbound as a pack of wolves flowed across the snow and up the Lamar Valley. The alpha male broke trail through 20-inch-deep snow and the other wolves followed in single file. Usually the followers stepped in his tracks, saving energy, but young wolves sometimes deviated from the trail to pounce and roll in the snow. Perhaps the snow helped cleanse their fur, perhaps snow cooled them off, or perhaps they were just playing.

Before us unfolded a magnificent wildlife story: the successful restoration of wolves to Yellowstone National Park and the Greater Yellowstone Ecosystem. Arguably the greatest wildlife experiment of the 20th century, restoration is a story of great achievement, a story of dedicated people, and a story of biological success. In this book, I will tell some stories of the wolves of Yellowstone, including some stories of the folks who look for wolves. (For books that detail the history of the restoration effort, please see "Recommended Reading" on page 97.)

Restoration of the wolf population has been successful beyond the greatest dreams of biologists, conservationists, and wolf enthusiasts. Little did we realize that Lamar Valley and the rest of Yellowstone National Park would become the showplace of wolf education and research. Nowhere else in the world (an impressive claim) have wolves been so visible, so studied, and so loved.

Yellowstone's Lamar Valley has been home to several wolf packs since the first wolves arrived in 1995. The open valley gives watchers an unprecedented view of a multitude of behavior interactions and carnivore ecology. During the eight years since restoration started, perhaps more wolves have been observed and more data collected here than in all past ecological research efforts. Now is the time to look back and ask, "What have we learned so far?"

In this book I have collected much of this new knowledge so that all may share in the excitement and success of this great wildlife experiment. Gathered here are answers to questions that I receive from students in my classes and from the public visiting Yellowstone. Gathered here are extraordinary photographs so that all may share in the beauty and awe of these wolves. All photos in this book are of wild, free Yellowstone wolves. Unlike so many wolf books, there are no pictures of captive wolves.

At dawn along Soda Butte Creek, a wolf, possibly 254M, gives an icy stare after howling at other wolves. Evidently not liking the message it received, the wolf trotted off in the opposite direction. Wolves are more easily seen in Yellowstone National Park than anywhere in the world. CINDY HARTMAN

INTRODUCTION

THE MAGIC OF YELLOWSTONE'S WOLVES

Large carnivores possess a "great magic" that captures and holds the minds of all who think about wilderness. We acknowledge the "magic" when we call the bears, cougars, and wolves, "charismatic megafauna."

I'm repeatedly amazed that in the cold hours before sunrise, I meet parents with little children along the road through Lamar Valley. They hope that come daylight, they may show their children a wolf. They come without binoculars, without spotting scopes, only with the hope that they may glimpse a wild, free-roaming wolf and pass that legacy to their children. How many of us remember that obligatory childhood visit to Yellowstone National Park? How many wish we could tell a story of seeing a wolf on that visit? That wish is now coming true for today's young wolf watchers.

Long ago I became hooked on charismatic megafauna and have made a life of seeking them in the far corners of the world. In 1990 I began to share the dream of observing wolves in the wild with others. Through my company, A Naturalist's World, we began teaching on-site, field classes about wolves. The classes were designed for anyone with interest—amateur naturalist, scientist, or wolf lover.

In those early years, our programs visited five locations for weeklong classes: Namadji National Forest, Ely, and Lutsen in Minnesota, and Banff and Jasper national parks in Canada. We tracked wolves, we studied them, and we looked. We worked hard, and the excitement, the "magic," was there to keep us going. I personally

taught eight five-day classes, 11 two-day seminars, and conducted research on 26 trips to different sites including Qinghai, China, while working with 26 biologists actively engaged in wolf research.

Even with the use of spotter planes and radio-collared wolves, only about twenty percent of my students ever saw even a fleeting glimpse of a wild wolf. Meanwhile in my front yard of Yellowstone National Park (I live in Gardiner, Montana), many dedicated people had succeeded in returning wolves to Yellowstone.

The first wolves were brought to Yellowstone in January 1995. I taught my first wolf class in Yellowstone the following March. Beginning with that class, every one of my Yellowstone classes through all the subsequent years has seen wild wolves.

In the early days, unaided by radios that have become commonplace for inter-car communications, we simply drove the park roads, looking carefully. Visitors learned to follow our vans because they knew we would locate wolves. Excitement and the "magic" compelled long hours. We looked from before daylight to after daylight. During the middle part of the day when the wolves slept, I taught wolf ecology. The first two winters that wolves were in Yellowstone, we saw wolves 85 percent of the mornings and 40 percent of the evenings that we looked for them. It was—and is—incredible.

Dedication is a word not lost on wolf watchers. One January morning it was 54 degrees below zero when Diann Thompson (my alpha female and co-owner of A Naturalist's World) and I led our class cross-country skiing across Lamar Valley. Out of the ice fog came the legendary figure of Jim Garry with his students. Jim is

Wolf watchers in Yellowstone have opportunities to recognize and learn about individual wolves. During the 2002 breeding season, this wolf, 113M from the Chief Joseph pack, entered Druid Peak pack territory, apparently trying to lure away a Druid female. One day he stood near the Yellowstone Association Institute and howled for more than an hour until 21M, the Druid alpha male, chased him away. BOB WESELMANN

chief liar (I smile when I use the term) of Lamar and curator of all things mythological and worthy of a good story. From Jim, we learn how native peoples around the world have viewed wolves and bears. Everyone should take a class with Jim.

As we visited, Jim told us that his class had spent the night huddled in sleeping bags in the main classroom of the Yellowstone Institute because the small propane heaters in the sleeping cabins could not keep them warm. Then, from deep in the ice fog, came a wolf howl. We never saw the wolf, only heard a lone howl. Hair stood on end. Smiles widened. Thumbs went up in a universal sign of success. That was the only wolf adventure that day, but we all retired elated.

The excitement of seeing wolves remains today. Not only do I still thrill at each glimpse I get, I revel in the excitement as people tell me the stories of their first sighting or even their latest sighting. Today I can get my "wolf fix" just by hearing the excitement of others.

Since that first class in March 1995, the number of wolf watchers has grown. In 2000, 57 classes in Lamar Valley had the word "wolf" in their titles. Wolf watchers are present from before dawn to after sunset, sleeping in the middle of the day. They come and stay for a month, two months, even three months at a time. Young students volunteer for the wolf study project and may stay more than a year. Many scientific studies by these volunteers have led to advanced academic degrees.

This book is an overview of the knowledge garnered by Yellowstone wolf watchers and, of course, some of their personal stories. Incidentally, I use the term "wolf watchers" in the broadest sense to include the person-on-the-road, the photographer, the videographer, the amateur naturalist, the manager, and the scientist. We are all watchers. This book is a "thank you" to all who have shared in the saga.

It was the public that made wolf restoration happen. It is my goal to share the people's success, the ongoing drama of wolves in Yellowstone.

KNOWING THE YELLOWSTONE WOLVES

The story of Yellowstone's wolves is a story of individual wolves and their families. To follow the story, we need to start with the first wolves to come to Yellowstone. In 1995 Diann and I realized the future complexity of monitoring and tracking individual wolves and packs, so we developed annual, color-coded charts to visually show genealogical relationships. Shown in this book are the charts for 1995, 1996, and 2002 (Appendices 1, 2 and 3). The 1995 and 1996 charts show the beginning of the project; the 2002 chart shows how far we have come.

Introductions began in 1995 with the importation of 14 wolves that were captured near Hinton, Alberta, Canada (see 1995 chart). Wolves arrived in two shipments on January 12 and 19. In 1996, 17 more wolves were brought to Yellowstone, this time from near Fort St. John, British Columbia, Canada (see 1996 chart). These wolves arrived on January 23 and 27.

THE FIRST WOLVES

It was recognized that the "unit" of wolf restoration was the pack, not individual wolves. After all, wolf recovery was predicated on establishing breeding packs in the ecosystem. Wolf packs are usually named after a prominent geographic feature within their territory.

Using the Lamar Valley as its territory has made the Druid Peak pack the most visible and most recognized wolf pack in the world. Much of what has been learned about Yellowstone's wolves derives from observations of this pack. Shown here are the five pack members that originally claimed control of the Lamar Valley. From left to right, they are 41F, 31M, alpha 38M, alpha 40F, and 42F. DAN HARTMAN

For Yellowstone, geographic and Native American names were used. Wolves that were reintroduced in 1995 comprised three packs: Crystal Creek, Rose Creek, and Soda Butte. Wolves that were reintroduced in 1996 comprised four packs upon release: Chief Joseph, Druid Peak, Lone Star, and Nez Perce. Pack names were derived from the location of the acclimation pens where wolves were kept for about 70 days before being released into the wild. The exception was the Chief Joseph pack named to honor the famous Nez Perce chief who led his people through Yellowstone in 1877.

Two other exceptions have been made. The first pack to form in the Yellowstone ecosystem is called the Leopold pack to honor the great conservationist, Aldo Leopold. In 1944 Leopold championed returning wolves to Yellowstone, even while they were being destroyed elsewhere.

Yellowstone wolf restoration would never have happened without the dedication and conviction of many people. One of the staunch supporters who even helped carry in the first wolves was Mollie Beattie, Director of the U.S. Fish and Wildlife Service. Without Mollie's work, there might not be wolves in Yellowstone. Fittingly, now that all the original wolves are gone from Crystal Creek pack, it has been renamed Mollie's pack.

During the summer of 1996, the founding Canadian wolves were supplemented with 10 wolf pups from a naturally recolonizing population near Augusta, Montana. The pups were born into the Sawtooth pack, and the pack subsequently killed some cattle. Several adult wolves were shot by Animal Damage Control agents. Ten of about 14 pups were captured and brought to Yellowstone where they were placed in the Nez Perce pen. (The Sawtooth wolves should not be confused with a captive pack by the same name that was owned by and featured in Jim and Jamie Dutcher's documentary, "Wolves at our Door.")

A total of 41 wolves constituting seven packs had been introduced into the Yellowstone ecosystem. Wolf recovery was predicated on establishing breeding packs with adequate genetic diversity to avoid problems from inbreeding, so the critical question became, "How many genetic stocks were brought to Yellowstone?"

Reintroductions came from three widely separated geographic areas. Wolves introduced in 1995 were known to have come from at least four packs, and wolves introduced in 1996 were known to have come from at least five packs. The Sawtooth wolves provided yet another genetic stock. Biologists believe that these diverse gene pools will provide an adequate genetic basis for future breeding.

As critical as genetic heritage is to the restoration process, so is behavior heritage. Considerable thought went into selecting areas from which wolves could be translocated to Yellowstone. One possible source was the wolf population in Minnesota. Bringing wolves from Minnesota would have been relatively easy because no international border would have to be crossed. But behavioral heritage was the deciding factor.

Wolves must learn to prey upon animals. It is a long learning process during which young wolves are highly dependent on association with and training by adult wolves. Indeed, perhaps part of the subsequent problems with livestock depredations by pups from the Sawtooth Pack may have been the lack of a training period as the pups grew up. After the pups were brought to Yellowstone, they spent most of a year in an acclimation pen before being released. The pups were not educated in how to kill wild animals, and perhaps this is why they turned more easily to livestock.

During the 2002 breeding season, 106F traveled as a lone wolf. Near Elk Creek, she howled to attract a mate. Not far away at Tower Junction, 113M howled an answer but the wolves did not get together. BOB WESELMANN

Biologists decided that the best wolves were ones that knew how to hunt Yellowstone prey. Minnesota wolves kill mostly deer and some moose. The wolves near Hinton, however, prey mainly on elk. The wolves near Fort St. John prey on elk primarily but occasionally kill bison. Thus we have Canadian wolves in Yellowstone.

KEEPING TRACK OF THE WOLVES

Wolf biologists need to know how many wolves are alive and where they are living in order to develop management plans and strategies. More importantly, the knowledge is needed to gauge the success or failure of restoration. However, finding a relatively small number of wolves in the approximately 15 million acres of the Greater Yellowstone ecosystem is a daunting task. Attaching radio collars to specific wolves facilitates locating wolf packs. As the population grows and territories expand, however, it is not possible to place a radio collar on every wolf. The ideal goal is to annually "collar" about half of the pups born each year and to recapture and re-collar the alpha wolves, the pack leaders, if necessary.

Collaring takes place in January and February, depending on the weather. Using helicopters, scientists from the Wolf Project locate wolves and fire a dart full of anesthesia into a selected wolf. Shortly after, the wolf goes into a sleep-like state. Researchers land the helicopter and attach a radio collar around the wolf's neck. They also check the wolf's health, age, gender, and weight, take blood samples, and inject antibiotics as a precaution against any effects from the dart wound. Pups must be nine months old or older to be collared. Younger pups would quickly outgrow a collar.

Federal funds for long-term research on the wolves are limited, and radio collars are expensive. About $400 buys a simple collar but state-of-the-art GPS (Global Positioning Satellite) collars cost thousands of dollars. To help defray the cost, the Yellowstone Park Foundation accepts public donations to "sponsor" a wolf collar. A $2,500 donation pays for a collar, the collaring activity, and for many other associated research activities.

Knowledge gained from radio-collared wolves and from a cadre of dedicated volunteer wolf watchers helps keep track of the number of wolves and their locations. The best time to evaluate population growth is just before pups are born each spring. The end-of-April or spring count represents the biological success of the preceding year. Immediately after pups are born in April the population is at its highest, but that high is short lived. Many pups and even some adults will die within the coming year.

POPULATION

Population growth (Appendix 6) has increased steadily since the beginning of restoration with the exception of 2000. Starting from a low of 14 in 1995, the population at the end of April 2002 was estimated at 200, although some uncollared, solitary wolves may not have been counted. Such wolves are difficult to find and may account for another 10 or 20 animals.

Net population growth represents the difference between the number born and the number that die each year. Net growth has added an average of 27 wolves to the population each year. The biological year 2000/2001 was the most successful with a net of 55 wolves added to the population, whereas the biological year 1999/2000 was the least successful with a net loss of 13 wolves.

Another way to evaluate restoration success is by counting the number of breeding packs. A conservative definition of a breeding pack is one that successfully raises through December the pups that were born that spring. On the average, two packs have been added each year (Appendix 7). In 1997 and 1999 no new packs were added, while eight new packs were found in 2002. There were about 25 groups—including true packs and small aggregations of wolves—in the ecosystem in 2002.

NUMBERS NOT NAMES

Scientists and wolf watchers refer to individual Yellowstone wolves by code numbers, not names. This tradition originated at the beginning of the project. Biologists and managers knew that there would be great interest in how the wolves were faring. School children were mesmerized by the process and wanted to adopt wolves to follow as their class mascot. However, biologists and managers suspected that a large number of wolves might die. The idea of a classroom of children adopting a wolf only to learn the next day that it had died was a grim specter.

Besides, names that humans might select would probably not reflect the way wolves see themselves. What would be a wolf name in the wolves' eyes? Would it be Spot, Blacky, John, or Natasha? Might wolves choose Swift Pursuer of Fleet Elk or something more appropriate? Rather than be anthropocentric, it was decided that out of respect, we should not name the wolves.

So the wolves of Yellowstone are known by individual numbers. They are numbered roughly in order of when they were captured. To indicate gender, a letter is added after the number, "M" for male and "F" for female. However, most of the time when we talk about a wolf, we simply say the number, such as 21, not 21M. In other words, in speech the gender indicator is silent, but in the written form the gender indicator is there to help our memories. As you read these accounts, it is easiest to simply think of a wolf by its number.

THE LESSONS LEARNED

The single most important lesson is to expect the unexpected. While we may be able to describe the "average" situation, trait, or behavior, there is great individual variation. Wolf watchers avoid single-factor answers and dogmatic explanations of "this is what it is." Biologists seek the complete picture with all its variations. Open your mind while you read this book because in Yellowstone we have learned many new lessons about wolves, providing great insight into a complex animal.

The first relocated wolves passed under Roosevelt Arch into Yellowstone National Park on January 12th, 1995. The watching world had little idea of the magnitude of the lessons to be learned, but an event on November 13, 1995, taught us how fortunate we were and how fortunate we would be in the coming years, if we were good students of the wolf.

Before daylight, cinematographer Bob Landis drove into the park. By nightfall, Bob returned with news and film that made our hearts skip. Bob had filmed the best-documented, most informative wolf hunting sequence ever. It has still not been surpassed.

As Bob watched, the Crystal Creek pack made a chase of elk on Jasper Ridge of Lamar Valley. It failed. They crossed Amethyst Creek and another spectacular chase ensued but in the trees. It failed. Bob was excited but frustrated. The wolves moved onto an alluvial fan of the river and two black yearlings, probably 2M and 6M, started to sift a herd of 30 to 40 elk.

The chase was developing in plain sight and relatively close. Bob knew his challenge. Movie cameras hold only 11 minutes of film before the film cartridge has to be changed, and in the cold November temperatures there is always the problem of camera batteries going dead. Bob started filming as the wolves came out of the trees. To his delight, the elk stayed in view. After a moment the wolves sensed a weak cow and singled her out. She was slower than the rest and ran with a limp. The cow fled, basically straight towards the camera. The wolves grabbed her by the neck and pulled

her to the ground. The kill was made, and there was still a smidgen of film left in the camera.

Two days later Wolf Project leader Doug Smith, myself, and our crew of biologists went to the elk carcass. There we discovered that the cow's rear leg was arthritic, the bones fused. The leg would not bend. The wolves knew, and the biologists learned.

Still, the magnitude of the chase hadn't sunk in. It took David Mech, the world's leading wolf biologist, to drive home the message. Dave told us Bob's film was "a breakthrough in terms of what we knew about wolves selecting their prey." Dave explained that he had spent his whole career trying to understand and prove how wolves select prey and which prey they kill. Until Bob's film, there was very little direct evidence that wolves actually select out those animals with lower ability. From other studies, biologists knew that wolves ended up with "weaker" animals, and the simplest explanation was that weak animals couldn't escape. But here was proof. Biologists could study the footage again and again. They could time all phases of the hunt.

Dave's comments had a bigger message. In Yellowstone, we were witnessing first hand "all the wonderful things" wolf biologists had dreamed about seeing—new populations with unlimited food supplies, reproductive stories, pack interactions, individual behavior, and much more. We learned we could identify wolves by their radio collars and coat colors, a breakthrough that opened the door to detailed observation and research.

Bob still ranks "The Chase" as his greatest event since he started filming in 1960. Of elk chases he says, "Yes, there are other good sequences, but they are too far, too dark, incomplete, or segmented. This is the only one I've ever filmed without turning off the camera at some point. It is the best documented of all kills."

The Chase was just a start on the lessons we've learned.

THE TERRITORIAL IMPERATIVE

Each wolf pack occupies and defends a territory where it actively advertises its presence by scent marking. Territories are dynamic entities, enlarging and shrinking in response to various factors. Abundant prey such as elk or deer may allow smaller territories to provide enough food for pack members. Successful reproduction produces more mouths to feed and may cause territory expansion. Deep or soft winter snowpack may reduce territory size. Conflict with a more aggressive, neighboring pack may shrink the territory.

TERRITORY SIZE

Biologists map the location of wolves over a time period to define the territory. However, some areas within the territory are used more and some areas used less. Therefore, we talk about an 85 percent territory size. The generalized maps shown in this book (Appendix 7) are about 85 percent approximations, or where you might find the wolves of a pack 85 percent of the time.

In Yellowstone, prey density, particularly of elk, is high, and pack territories have been relatively small. Territory size has varied from about 35 square miles to about 800 square miles. The average wolf territory has probably been around 300 square miles, compared to Alaska where territories may be as large as 5,000 square miles.

As Yellowstone's wolf population has grown, territories have spread across the map. While territory size and therefore the number of territories may vary, the ecosystem can only support so many territories. The yearly maps show how full the ecosystem is. The 2002 map shows the northern half of the ecosystem to be relatively full and the key question is, "How many more territories are available?"

Probably the most important characteristic of a territory is its food supply, especially during the harsh mountain winter. Seemingly unused areas to the northeast and southwest of the park may not be suitable for wolves. The high-elevation volcanic plateaus in the northeast and the heavily logged regions of Targhee National Forest to the southwest currently do not support large elk populations in the winter. Few wolf packs will probably ever become established in those areas. There are only eight wintering grounds for elk around Yellowstone National Park and a few smaller ones south along the Wind River Mountains. Comparison of existing territories with winter ranges suggests that the limit to the number of territories is drawing near.

Predicting exactly how many territories there will eventually be is difficult. I'll hazard a guess that the number of packs will probably not double from their current number. However, competition might force packs to have fewer members and smaller territories, so the number of packs might increase while the total number of wolves levels out.

SCENT MARKING

Territories are bounded by a nebulous border, called by some the "no wolf zone." This border region often shifts, both in geographic location and width, and wolves often venture into boundary areas. Each pack patrols the borders of its territory, defecating and urinating along the way, leaving a scent signal to warn other packs to stay out. Scent marking is most intense along the borders and major travel routes within the territory. Some areas within the territory may not be visited often by pack members.

Along the Firehole River, a lodgepole pine forest provides cover for a hunter from the Nez Perce pack. This pack's territory lies north and east of Old Faithful. In 2002 the Yellowstone area supported 200 wolves and 25 packs and groups an astonishing increase from 13 wolves and 3 packs released in 1995. Pack territories are dynamic, shifting in size and boundaries according to such factors as food supply, pack size, and weather. JESS R. LEE

The first line of territorial defense is to prevent conflict during which you might get hurt. Wolves adhere to this rule steadfastly. Territorial marking tells others, "Stay out!" But there are many nuances to the marking process that non-odor-oriented humans (we're visually oriented) do not appreciate. Much of the wolf's skull contains odor receptors, not only in the nose but also in the mouth. The wolf, if you will, "sees" with its nose.

To better understand what it means to "see" with your nose, Jim Garry suggests imagining your vision behaving in the same way as odor reception. A single sniff not only tells the wolf who was here but how long ago they passed. A person would see another person, but the faintness of the image would tell the passage of time. We would look back on the trail continually seeing the person; the image would get fainter going away. Looking up the trail the image would become clearer. In some spots of favorable "seeing," we might catch glimpses of a person who had passed days ago, even weeks. Not only might our vision tell us the sex of the person, but also his or her reproductive condition and maybe even something about their position in the social dominance hierarchy.

Kerry Murphy, cougar and wolf researcher in Yellowstone, remembers observing wolves "seeing" an intruder with their nose. Kerry is a special field biologist who has lived and hiked much of the backcountry of Yellowstone while trailing his study animals. First a cougar specialist, Kerry became the wolf biologist for the Wolf Project, and today he and I even track Canada lynx in the backcountry.

The alpha male of a group nicknamed the "Norris Three" looks over his shoulder from a point above the Norris Geyser Basin. Steam from some of the basin's hot springs and geysers rises beyond the wolf. The Norris Three were often seen in this area in 2002 and 2003, perhaps establishing a new territory. BOB WESELMANN

In mid-November 1999, Kerry and others watched the Druid Peak pack travel from Specimen Ridge down into Antelope Creek. Reports from biologists in planes that morning had told them that two radio-collared members of the Rose Creek pack had crossed to the upper slopes of Antelope Creek.

As Kerry watched, Druid Peak wolves encountered the snow trail left by the Rose Creek wolves. Druid Peak members took great interest in the trail and milled about while sniffing and discerning who had past that way. Suddenly they gained initiative and exploded up the trail. At a full gallop, Druid Peak wolves climbed to within a quarter mile of the top of Mount Washburn. There they either lost interest or lost the trail and came back down.

In May 1999 Kerry was watching the den of 9F north of Lamar River in a region known as Mom's Ridge. The alpha male and prominent members of the pack had been gone for at least 16 hours, perhaps on a hunting trip. As Kerry watched, one of the den's yearling wolves caught his eye about a quarter mile away. The wolf was sniffing the ground, but Kerry could not determine why. Finally the yearling seemed to pick up a scent direction and slowly began to move off. The youngster had picked up the old, weak scent of the adults and was setting out to find them. The nose knows!

A wolf needs to scent mark close enough together so that its urine odor forms a scent fence along the territory border. The odor needs to be dispersed by the wind so it must be placed high on an object. Wolves (and dogs) do this by raised leg urination or called RLU by behaviorists. They are claiming their territory as top dog.

Since wolves can recognize individuals by their urine odor, it is important for alpha animals to keep subordinates from urinating high on objects and implying alpha status. Therefore, alpha animals make subordinates squat to urinate. Remember both the alpha male and the alpha female wolves do a RLU, but subordinates of both sexes squat (SQU). Wolves also can identify sex by odor, especially at times of the year when the female is in estrus.

Incidentally, alpha wolves must ration their urine. If the wolf used all its urine at one spot, territory marking would take forever. Alpha wolves only use a little urine, sometimes even just drops, each time they mark. A large urine stain in the snow with wolf footprints on each side indicates a subordinate. When following trails during the winter, I have found that the wolves tend to scent mark about every 0.25 to 0.38 miles. Feces or scat can also be used to reinforce the territorial marking. Perhaps scat retains its odor longer than urine.

Let's not rule out the importance of subordinate markings. Although subordinates tend to mark in the main trail and not high on objects, intruders may be able to "count" the number of wolves urinating in a territory and even "judge" the size of a pack. I don't mean to imply that wolves can actually count, but biologist do know that some animals have number sense and can judge smaller and larger numbers of things. Perhaps scent markings indicate more or less wolves. I am sure wolves communicate more with their odors then we will ever comprehend.

Odor from both urine and scat eventually dissipates, so scent markers must be replenished frequently. Consequently, piles of scat of differing ages may be found at a marking point. Wolves also repeatedly urinate in the same spot.

In Yellowstone scent marking tends to be densest along the most commonly used trails, usually along the valley floor, and not necessarily along the borders of territories. Wolves also travel on the park's main roads at night and scent mark high on snow banks. Often, I have followed wolf tracks up to these banks to find nose prints in the snow. Upon excavating the snow under the print, I have found old, urine-soaked snow. Evidently, the odor not only lingers for an extended period but also passes through the snow.

TERRITORIAL BATTLES

Sometimes the scent warnings don't work and wolves must defend their territories. Defense of a territory is critical because possession guarantees access to prey resources, especially if resources are scarce. From advertising to fighting, all pack members probably play a role, even if only by the presence of their body odors.

Packs vigorously defend their territories. The first great territorial battle probably occurred in October 1995. The Rose Creek pack had just been released from its pen for the second time. The original alpha male 10M had been illegally shot earlier in the year, and a new alpha pair had formed, 9F and 8M.

Famed wildlife cinematographer Bob Landis looked south from the road to Amethyst Bench in the Lamar Valley and spotted the Crystal Creek pack coming from the east. Bob remembers Crystal yearlings 2M, 3M, and 6M attacking first, catching 9F and possibly pinning her to the ground. Then the Crystal pack spotted all ten members of the Rose Creek pack, but little did they know that eight of the wolves were pups—not much good in a fight. At sight of the larger pack, Crystal members 4M and 5F turned tail and started to run, but 9F was still in trouble.

Now 8M had to choose loyalties. Wolves 2M, 3M, and 6M were his siblings with which he had sent most of the summer. But 9F was his new partner. Without hesitation, 8M turned on his kin and chased them back across Amethyst Bench. It appeared 8M may have even caught one and dealt it a disciplining bite.

In 1999 the Druid Peak pack dealt harshly with a territorial infringement by 85F, a Rose Creek wolf. The Druids caught and killed 85F. Fifteen Yellowstone wolves have died as the result of territorial battles, even though wolves try to avoid conflicts by scent marking territory boundaries. DOUGLAS SMITH/NPS

The Druid Peak pack is famous for killing wolves that stray into its territory. In such incidents, strategy is important, but the bottom line is that the pack with the most active fighters is usually the winner. For example, on June 21, 1996, the Druid Peak pack encountered the Rose Creek pack. A month earlier the Druids had successfully vanquished the Crystal Creek pack and killed the alpha male 4M. On this occasion, however, the Rose pack had more members (9 wolves) than Druid Peak (5 wolves), and Druid Peak was soundly beaten, with the alpha female, 39F, barely escaping by fleeing into the river. Nonetheless, as the Druid Peak pack fled, a young adult (20M) from Rose Creek evidently pursued them beyond the help of his pack mates and was killed when the odds changed.

The concept of active fighter is important. Numbers alone may not confer success in a battle. It appears that a wolf must be at least a year old before it can be a significant force in a battle. In 2001 we observed the Rose Creek pack again rout the Druid Peak pack, which had more members but only five adults at the time. Usually the outnumbered wolf or wolves will turn and run. As a result, wolves often receive wounds to their hindquarters and rumps. Sometimes severely wounded wolves may survive and heal. When Druid Peak pack attacked the Crystal Creek pack in 1996, 5F's mate, 4M, was killed and she was severely wounded. 5F limped around with her back hunched and her head held low. Her son, 6M, caught food for both of them. They moved to Pelican Valley where 5F recovered.

Some territorial disputes involve the need to expand a territory because a pack has grown so large that food may be limiting. The best example of this occurred following the 2000 pup season when the Druid Peak pack grew to 26 wolves. Druid Peak expanded their territory west through Slough Creek to past Hellroaring Creek, all areas claimed by the Rose Creek pack. The Rose Creek pack fragmented with a small group staying in the Tower Falls/Roosevelt area and the rest moving northwest to the edge of the park.

Fifteen Yellowstone wolves have been killed as the result of territorial battles. 35M was found where he had tried to take cover under a log. Another wolf may have been chased into an avalanche zone where it was caught in an avalanche. If 19F was killed by the Druid Peak pack, then the loss of her four pups to starvation counts as an indirect loss to interpack conflict.

The urge to defend the pack is strong. Doug Smith, leader of the Yellowstone Wolf Project, points to male behavior when biologists in helicopters try to dart wolves to place radio collars around their necks. Females are often the first to run and they head into the densest timber available. Younger wolves quickly follow. However, the males, especially the alpha male, will often stand defiantly ready to defend the pack. By remaining in the open, they are easy targets for the biologists.

The urge of males to defend may help explain the interpack conflict deaths of seven males but only four females. Importantly, one alpha male, 4M, may have been killed trying to defend its territory.

At times, retreat may be the best strategy. On March 26, 1997, the Druid Peak pack (5 wolves) found themselves caught off-guard by the Rose Creek pack (8 wolves). Druid Peak beat a hasty retreat back to the east, running parallel to the road until they disappeared over the ridgetop 3.2 miles from the encounter. We were able to observe the retreat and later track the wolves through the snow. While the snow surface was mostly hard, the wolves often broke through the crust.

In spite of the difficult snow conditions, the wolves achieved remarkable speeds for extended distances. Alpha female 40F covered the 3.2 miles in 8 minutes for a speed of 24 miles per hour. Additionally 40F climbed and descended over 500 vertical feet. The alpha male, 38M, covered the distance in less time, but we were not able to ascertain when he disappeared and could not estimate his speed. The females 41F and 42F were traveling besides each other. One of them traveled 1.7 miles at 20.4 miles per hour and three miles at 12.9 miles per hour. One female covered 13 feet per stride (from where one foot touches the ground to where the same point on the same foot touches the ground again) at the 1.7-mile mark. I estimate that a fresh wolf in a hurry can cover 25 feet per stride.

It is interesting that neither 38M nor 40F waited for the rest of the pack. Females 41F and 42F lagged considerably behind as their leaders left. 31M became separated from the pack and remained on

River crossings are a way of life for wolves. Some crossings are smooth, some are quick, and a few are fatal. Four wolves have been found dead in Yellowstone's streams and rivers. Exploratory forays often require river crossings. Here a Nez Perce wolf finds easy swimming in the Firehole River. JESS R. LEE

a hill howling for pack mates. In this case, the alphas used their superior physical abilities to quickly outdistance the rest of the pack.

Wolves will retreat into rivers to escape pursuers. This was the case when 39F escaped into Slough Creek as the Rose Creek Pack attacked on June 21, 1996. However, a water escape doesn't always work. 189M was found dead in Tom Miner Creek where it had apparently been chased by other wolves. The ultimate cause of death was drowning.

Another defense might be deception. Some have suggested that wolves roll in smelly objects (such as scat or a carcass) to hide their odor. I doubt that this maneuver can fool the exquisite nose of a wolf. More likely, the wolf perceives the scenario as, "Here comes Joe and he's been rolling in bison scat."

Another suggested hypothesis is that the wolf is trying to override the odor of a rival. To me this is a less compelling hypothesis as both urine and feces have a stronger odor than the rival's body. To dominate a rival wolf's odor, it would make more sense to urinate or defecate on the rival's scat.

Scent rolling might also convey some advantage while hunting. Rolling in the scat or carcass of an elk or bison might hide the wolf's odor. Then a closer approach might be possible before starting a chase. However, deception is probably not the reason for scent rolling behavior.

A more probable explanation for scent-roll behavior is that it is used for communication. Perhaps while scouting, a lone wolf finds an elk carcass. By rolling on the carcass, the wolf may carry home a scent message that it not only found an elk carcass but that carcass was only three days old. Other wolves could weigh their hunger versus freshness and probably quantity (a fresh smelling carcass might have more meat left) to decide if they should return to the find. Forgive me for anthropomorphizing, but wolves do somehow evaluate information. Rolling in a scat would communicate the animal species that defecated, its sex, reproductive status, and the time delay since defecation. Do not underestimate the power of wolf odor communications.

EXPLORATORY FORAYS

Since territories are large, a pack cannot mark and defend all areas of the territory at all times. Packs tend to "prefer" a central area. Additionally, wolves will often make exploratory forays far from the central area, even 50 or more miles.

Perhaps the leading contender for foray king is 253M. Sometime in late October or early November 2002, 253M started exploring. At some point he may have been joined by another gray wolf. On November 30, 2002, 253M was caught in a coyote trap southwest of Ogden, Utah, a journey with a straight-line distance of approximately 175 miles. The journey is even more remarkable in that 253M was limping on a hind leg that became crippled after a territorial battle with the Nez Perce pack in October 2002.

U.S. Fish and Wildlife Services biologist Mike Jiminez picked up 253M in Utah and transported him to Grand Teton National Park, where he was released. On December 20, 253M was located in Yellowstone's Lamar Valley, traveling with his old pack, the Druids. Now 253M was also limping on a front foot but keeping up with the pack. Perhaps it was the long journey, perhaps it was the trap that caused the limp, but nonetheless 253M was home. The total journey, by any reckoning, must have been more than 400 miles.

Exploratory behavior often occurs in the fall and early spring. Fall forays may serve to show pups their new homes. In the spring, the snowpack turns hard as daytime snowmelt freezes at night. The melt-freeze process forms smooth, firm, snow highways to travel great distances.

HUNTING AND PREDATION

Yellowstone's Lamar Valley has proven to be the Utopia for observing interactions between wolves and their prey. Deep winter snows on the mountains drive prey animals down into the valley, where the wolves are waiting. The open valley, crossed by the only park road that stays open to cars all winter, provides unprecedented chances to see and study wolves hunting.

THE WINTER STUDY

In 1995 Mike Phillips, Doug Smith, Bob Crabtree, and I designed an initial strategy for what quickly evolved into "Winter Study." The original plan was to locate wolves on Day One and again on Day Two. But after locating the wolves on Day Two so we knew where they were, we would go back to the Day One location and then back track the wolves' trail, learning everything we could from the trails, signs, and carcasses. The tracking strategy was designed to prevent interference with the daily activities of the wolves.

Central to our strategy was the plan Doug designed, in consultation with his long-time mentor and friend Rolf Peterson (leading scientist and authority on the wolves of Isle Royale). This plan took the best ideas from the Isle Royale studies, and even from Alaskan studies, to craft a study specific for Yellowstone. If possible, every animal killed by the wolves or a carcass used by the wolves would be located and analyzed. Biologists would glean information about species and gender. By retrieving a jawbone, prey could be aged by counting annual growth rings in their teeth. Nutritional status could be determined by cutting through a long bone, ideally the femur, and checking fat content in the bone marrow. Determinations also would be made as to whether the animal was killed by hunting or simply scavenged after some other form of death.

On November 14, 1995, Doug Smith, Dan MacNulty, Chase Davis, Nathan Varley, and I put the plan to work. Well, almost. Snows were late coming that fall, and there was hardly a trace of snow on the Lamar Valley floor. This meant tracking would be difficult and slow, not a tolerable situation when one is trying to follow the far-reaching activities of a day in the lives of wild wolves. The plan had to be modified: forget tracking. Winter Study evolved into a ground and aerial observation program collecting data on every carcass that could be retrieved.

Doug designed Winter Study with two study periods. One looked at prey populations that were only mildly stressed by environmental conditions (early winter). The second period studied prey animals that were heavily stressed (late winter). In early winter, November 15 to December 15, the prey, usually elk, have large reserves of fat and can still find grass to feed on. By late winter, the month of March, prey are using their fat reserves, often severely depleting them, and food is very scarce.

The two study periods provide excellent glimpses into the world of hunting by wolves. Success of both predator and prey changes between periods. Each must develop a strategy of survival.

STRATEGIES OF WOLVES AND THEIR PREY

Consider the wolf. A big wolf, a really big wolf, weighs 130 pounds. An average bull elk weighs 750 pounds, a cow elk 520 pounds, and a calf 220 pounds. Let me put this in human terms. Did you ever pick a

Near Slough Creek, a hillside of tan rumps signals a fleeing herd of elk as three Druid Peak wolves give chase. By repeatedly dividing a herd and testing individual animals—a process described as "sifting and sorting"—wolves try to find and isolate weak or slower animals. Most chases end without a kill, but this time the wolves were successful. The chase lasted about two minutes. PETE BENGEYFIELD

fight with someone six times your size? That is what a wolf does when it attacks a bull elk. So wolves compensate by using hunting strategies that include locating, observing, stalking, testing, and maneuvering.

Wolves stalk just like a house cat does. Wolves on the opposite side of a small hill from elk will stand on their hind legs to peer over the top while their bodies remain concealed. Once visual contact is made, wolves often move into cover to try to get closer. Wolves may even lay on their bellies and crawl forward under cover of tall grass. They will walk in a slinking posture, lowering their visual profile. When stalking, wolves may pause every step. If an elk is watching they do not move until the elk looks away. The strategy is to get as close as possible before starting a chase.

Most chases are tests to determine if there is a weaker animal in a group. Wolves will run into a herd of elk, splitting the herd. Then the wolves will run into one of the subgroups, splitting the subgroup. Testing may last a long time with wolves moving at top speed. Doug Smith describes wolves as "sifters and sorters."

During early winter, about 80 percent of chases ended without wolves making a kill. In late winter when elk were nutritionally depleted, about 70 percent of chases ended without a kill. Wolves fail most of the time.

If a weak animal is spotted, the wolves' strategy depends on how the elk is behaving. Killing elk is dangerous, and at least two wolves, 6M and 14F, may have died from a kick by an elk or moose. Wolf strategy involves an unconscious evaluation of risk to be in the safest position relative to the prey while making a kill.

If the elk is running, the number of wolves that can be closely involved in a kill is limited. The most dangerous place for a wolf is directly behind an elk, within reach of its flailing hind hooves. A straight back hind-hoof kick is more dangerous than a hind-hoof kick to the side. Therefore, if an elk is running, the safest places are to the sides, limiting the number of prime pursuers to two, one on each side. It is safest for a wolf to bite the throat. If the elk kicks at the wolf, the kick is from the front feet, up and either forward or out to the side. The front kick is not as deadly as one directly back from the hind feet. Consequently, many kills of running elk are made by one or two wolves.

The relative safety of positions to bite an elk may depend on its gender. Doug Smith reports that wolves apparently can be more easily injured hanging onto the throat of a large bull elk and therefore tend to grab bulls by the hindquarters while running alongside. Wolves often grab cow elk by the throat.

If the elk stands its ground, the strategy is different. A standing elk can rear up on its hind feet to strike its front feet down on the wolf, perhaps fracturing the spine or skull. The safest strategy is to get behind, but slightly to the side of, the elk and grab its

The Druid Peak pack made an elk kill north of Soda Butte. After feeding, most of the pack went into the forest to sleep, but this yearling came back to the carcass to eat some more. After feeding, the wolf went to the base of Druid Peak and slept. DONALD M. JONES

hindquarters, hampering its mobility. Perhaps a second wolf can grab the elk by the throat. Evidently an elk can turn fast enough to ward off not only one but two wolves. However, when a third wolf joins the hunt, the elk quickly ends up with its back end facing a set of fangs. If one wolf has grabbed the hindquarters, the other wolves generally make a throat bite.

Killing bites are almost always to the throat. The long, sharp canine teeth allow the wolf to secure a good hold and hang on. Generally the windpipe is crushed and the animal dies of asphyxiation. The idea that the wolf is going for the jugular vein is not true. In most cases, the jugular vein is not damaged. Canine teeth puncture and hold but do not cut well.

Wolves bite not only to kill but also to weaken and disable. Failed hunts may result in disabling bites that allow the wolves to return another time to complete the kill. I watched as one large bull elk successfully warded off several wolves, but the bull was bitten several times mostly on the hindquarters. The bull was too injured to leave the area and simply stood there. When the wolves returned a day later, the bull had stiffened up due to its wounds and the wolves soon killed it.

Wolves may also use sneak attacks. Deb Guernsey, a wolf biologist, has spent many lone, quiet hours observing wolves as part of her job. Deb has twice observed 17F try a sneak attack. Both times, 17F was ahead of her Rose Creek pack when the pack started to chase elk herds. 17F hid in some trees and waited. As the herd approached, 17F waited until the last minute to spring from cover and attack. She was young and never did get an elk, but maybe the strategy worked better when she became older, bigger, and faster.

The elk are not simply pawns in this deadly game of predation. Elk have strategies too, and these depend on their nutritional status. Dan MacNulty, wolf biologist, has shown that elk may communicate to the wolves that they are fit and ready to fight. Especially in early

Druid Peak wolves attack a large bull elk in the Lamar Valley. Seventy to eighty percent of wolf hunts fail, but this January morning the Druids were successful. The battle lasted about five minutes. In hunting, wolves seek whatever opportunities are presented by the prey's old age, young age, poor nutrition, bad health, deep snow, or, sometimes, just bad luck. PETE BENGEYFIELD

winter when calories are abundant, elk, especially cows, show off their fitness by a prancing, heads-up trot. The head is held with the chin slanting up above horizontal and the neck is thrust forward and out. Legs are raised to a slightly exaggerated height and the elk trots instead of gallops. Normally when trotting the chin is below horizontal and the neck is not thrust out. The exaggerated posture seems to convey the message that the cow is strong, ready, and willing to fight. Additionally, in a straight race a cow using this trot often outdistances a wolf. Wolves testing elk will avoid a cow behaving in this manner.

In early winter, elk often lead wolves on long, unsuccessful chases. When wolves do make a successful kill, it often takes several minutes to bring the elk to the ground.

In late winter, elk do not have the energy necessary to flee great distances. Additionally, snow may be deep and thick drifts can mire down even a large bull. Therefore, elk tend not to flee but to stand and fight. If possible, elk will move short distances to bare ground:

a bare knob where wolves are downhill on all sides is preferred. Several elk will form bands or loose circles. Another strategy is to back up against a tree.

Elk usually defend themselves by kicking. For cows and bulls, the preferred kick is to rise up on hind legs and come down on the wolf with the front legs. However, an elk can use a single front leg to kick forward, sideways, and back. The back kick by the hind legs is particularly powerful and can be done while galloping away from the wolves. Elk also posses a "secret" kick, which is the backwards kick by a hind leg while feigning not looking. During this maneuver, the elk's chin is raised high and the elk, whose eyes are at the side of the head, looks backwards and down over its own hindquarters to see where the wolf is. We watched as a bull elk nearly ended the career of a yearling from Druid Peak pack with a near miss while using this deadly kick. Even for bulls, kicking is the most efficient defense mechanism. Although bull elk have impressive sets of pointed antlers with considerable power behind them, bulls usually do not try to fend off wolves with their antlers.

Doug Smith points out that wolves don't just kill any animal, any time they wish. Hunting is dangerous. Six wolves have died while hunting, five hunting elk and one hunting a moose. Doug remembers 14F, a wolf that arrived in 1995 with Soda Butte Pack. She was later moved south of the Southeast Arm of Yellowstone Lake to serve as a founder of the Delta pack. Mother of three litters, 14F was an experienced hunter and relatively large for a female at 104 pounds. Nonetheless, during a moose hunt, the moose ended her life.

Another prey defense strategy is the water escape. Marc Catellier shared the following story with me. A registered nurse and high-wire walker in a past life, Marc is now a caterer, musician, conservationist, bison supporter, prospector, and Yellowstone mentor.

Just after daylight in April 2002, Marc was helping me teach a wolf class for members of Defenders of Wildlife. He had parked his car on the road just east of the Yellowstone Institute and stepped out when an elk appeared on the hill above him. The bull fled down the steep hill at breakneck and break-leg speed. Desperate, the elk came towards Marc as 21M crested the hill in hot pursuit. Marc watched as the steep hill slowed 21M, giving the elk more lead. As the elk brushed by Marc, he saw blood on the elk's hind legs. 21M had already made contact.

Across the road in the flats, 21M caught up to the elk and again grabbed a rear leg but was shaken off. Finally the bull gained the Lamar River and plunged in. Quickly the bull waded into water chest deep. 21M came to the riverbank and stopped. In the deep water the bull was a formidable opponent. 21M was stymied.

21M paced the riverbank, then swam to the other side where he paced some more. He waded into water up to his chest but did not attack. Out again, he paced the shore. Then 21M returned to Marc's side of the river and lay down to rest.

It became a cycle: swim the river, test the water, swim the river, rest, do it all again. If the elk came close to shore, 21M got ready to pounce but the bull retreated to deeper water. And so it went for several hours. Finally 21M went back up the hill to where the chase began hours earlier. Later in the day, 21M and 42F came down the hill and headed west with scarcely a look at the bull. When we last saw the bull at twilight, it was still in the river.

Morning revealed the rest of the story. On the river's edge lay the bull. Its carcass had fed several wolves. We'll never know what happened, but the river defense had worked for awhile. Did the bull grow weary during the night and leave the water? Did wolves eventually enter the water to attack a hypothermic, battle-weakened elk? The dark of the night held the secret of the bull's final demise.

"Snow is the great equalizer in the hunting process," says Dan MacNulty. Cross-country ski lover that he is, Dan has pondered the role of snow in the hunting process. Dan compares the wolf/prey interaction to a teeter-totter. Snow depth serves as the teeter-totters's fulcrum. Shifting that fulcrum can benefit one species or the other. As animals move, that fulcrum can shift in an instant.

To illustrate his point, Dan relates the first complete bison hunt he witnessed near Yellowstone Lake. It was March 17, 1999, and he was watching a herd of about 150 bison interact with 15 wolves in an area where deep snow separated areas of bare ground like beads on a string. That morning Dan saw the wolves do a group howl and then proceed directly to the bison. The wolves seemed absolutely intent on killing a bison. It took over nine hours, but with the help of the snow the wolves made their kill.

During the day it was a back and forth battle. The wolves would charge the bison and the bison would charge the wolves. While the bison were on snow-free hills, the wolves could not gain an advantage. It became a waiting game, but bison would only stay on a patch of ground so long. Dan speculates that waiting was a function of the amount of grass on a patch, the number of bison, and hunger. Eventually the grass in an area would be eaten. Then bison stress increased and dominance interactions elevated. Eventually the bison would make a break for the next patch of snow-free ground.

The only routes were narrow trails of hoof-packed snow. On either side of these trails was deep, treacherous snow that could trap a bison that left the trails. Considerable jostling occurred and any bison knocked off the trail or the last bison in line fell victim to the biting wolves. On every passage between patches, the wolves would bite

Two Druid Peak wolves pause as they feed on an elk calf. Young elk make up a high percentage of elk killed by wolves. Of course, elk calves are also vulnerable to mountain lions, grizzly bears, and coyotes.
DONALD M. JONES

After feeding on an elk carcass with other members of the Druid Peak pack, 224M rears up in an attempt to pounce on a mouse or vole beneath the snow. More than other wolves, 224M often "moused" after a kill. Was the behavior just play or were the mice dessert? DAN HARTMAN

and hang on to an unlucky bison. A strong bison would drag as many as ten wolves to the new patch. Then three or four bison would swarm the wolves, chasing them off. The bison that helped would not expose themselves by going into the snow. They would only help when their fellow bison reached snow-free ground.

Finally what appeared to be a three-year-old cow was last to cross. This time enough wolves grabbed hold to prevent her from getting to snow-free ground and the wolves had their meal. The next day a grizzly took the carcass from the wolves.

In late winter, elk kills happen quickly, often in less than a minute. Jennifer Sands was up the Lamar River in late 2000 collecting samples for her wolf study. She didn't know that 21M was returning to the same area. Into the river bottom came 21M, where she saw him. She said all she could think about was "don't move, don't disturb him!"

As Jennifer watched, 21M approached along the river bottom but on a high ridge. 21M spotted a cow elk and went directly toward it, coming within about 100 yards of Jennifer. There was a lot of undergrowth between them and 21M either did not know Jennifer was there or did not care. He was locked on the cow.

The cow was by herself. She and 21M circled each other for a long time, each trying for the superior position in this pending life or death struggle. The rapidity of what happened next surprised Jennifer. There was no chase. With a quick lunge to the neck 21M grabbed hold and held on. The cow continued circling and twirling, trying to shake the wolf loose, but to no avail. Within a minute, it was over. As Jennifer watched, slowly each member of the 21M's Druid Peak pack materialized out of nowhere to share the meal. Rapid kills indicate winter-weakened elk.

The final element in the hunting equation is risk evaluation. Dan MacNulty believes that wolf hunting behavior revolves around the need to kill prey without being killed. He says the concept of wolves killing the most vulnerable prey is an incomplete explanation of what is happening. Vulnerable prey animals generally are older, sicker, and weaker animals, but they are selected because they are safer to kill.

Dan believes wolves, in effect, evaluate the risk of being gored, kicked, or otherwise harmed and select prey that are less likely to harm them. Behavioral sensitivity to risk is reflected in wolves taking greater numbers of less-dangerous elk than they take of more-dangerous bison. If bison are the only available prey animals, wolves accommodate for the increased risk by patiently waiting and looking for the best opportunity. Wolf hunting behavior is a function not only of vulnerability but perhaps more importantly, risk reduction.

Yellowstone wolves kill almost exclusively elk. The cost-versus-benefit-versus-risk ratio of killing an elk is great. Elk are large enough to provide ample food for many wolves, often for several days. However, an elk is not as big, strong, and dangerous as a bison, so the probability of injury is lower. The number of buffalo killed since 1995 is probably less than 45. Other prey species may be less dangerous but provide less return per effort and seem to be taken less frequently. For example, Yellowstone wolves are known to have killed only about 27 deer, 8 pronghorn antelope, 1 bighorn sheep, 1 mountain goat, and 1 beaver.

When feeding, Yellowstone wolves first open the belly of a carcass, allowing the stomach and intestines to fall on the ground. They first eat the large muscles of the front quarters and hindquarters and the major organs, the heart, liver, and lungs. Lastly, muscle is chewed off ribs, leg bones, and the hide. Muscles and organs are easy to eat, but it is more difficult to obtain meat from other parts of the body.

Researchers Chris Wilmers and Dan Stahler have found that wolves have a feeding rate of about 2.4 pounds per minute of muscle or organ, but only 0.6 pounds per minute from ribs, legs, and hide.

Early morning hunts along rivers provide access to waterfowl and anything that might wash up during the night. Though on the far side of the Firehole River, this Nez Perce wolf shows its curiosity for the photographer. Short summer fur allows wolves to remain cool and emphasizes their relatively long legs. JESS R. LEE

Consider, for a moment, the implications of the wolf's high feeding rate. Given ten minutes to feed, a wolf could eat 20 pounds of food. To accommodate the high feeding rate, wolves have stomachs that expand to accommodate extra large meals. Ten wolves could quickly remove 200 pounds of meat from a carcass. Think about how fast the Druid Peak pack, having upwards of 30 wolves, could devour a carcass.

At a kill site, biologists carefully perform a necropsy, a wild animal autopsy, to determine if extenuating circumstances increased the vulnerability of a prey animal. The necropsy is a powerful tool for it may reveal diseases or old injuries which wolves sensed in selecting the animal.

U.S. Fish and Wildlife Service biologist David Mech, simply one of the greatest wolf biologists ever, has spent his whole career studying wolves and necropsying prey animals. Dave told me that only so many kinds of disabilities are evident in a pile of bones and fur. In fact, some disabilities might not be evident even if we were standing next to the live animal. Dave asks, "What can a carcass tell us about the animal's vision, hearing, or even intelligence?"

Simple bad luck may occasionally play a role. I have watched as wolves chased and bit elk at the trailing end of a fleeing herd. When the front end of the herd slowed down, the cows at the back of the herd ran into a solid wall of elk butts, and the wolves took advantage. Elk sometimes flee into or are chased into deep pockets of snow where their narrow feet fail to hold their weight. The elk sink until their bellies stop additional downward movement. The relatively large feet of the wolves allow them to remain on top of the snow and attack the elk without being kicked.

Dave Mech points out that the larger the prey, the better it may be equipped to reverse the effect of a bad-luck encounter. A snowshoe hare coming around a rock into the path of an approaching wolf may be out of luck, but a healthy bull elk might escape.

PREDATION ON ELK

Elk are not only of prime importance as a food source to wolves, they are critical players in the economy of the Greater Yellowstone ecosystem. Some hunters are concerned that wolf predation might create substantial losses of hunting opportunity and income. Those of us who support wolves would do well to remember that the dollars that come into Montana from hunting are responsible for most wildlife and much habitat management. Montana, a state at the bottom of per capita income, would be in poor shape without hunter dollars. Local economies and people depend on hunting seasons, both for food and dollars. The interaction between wolves and game animals must be carefully monitored and controlled.

The Northern Yellowstone elk herd is perhaps the largest migratory herd in the world, numbering 10,000 to 20,000 animals. While most animals are summer residents in the high country of Yellowstone, many migrate down and out of the park during difficult winter months. A special hunting season, called the Late Hunt, was established to control elk numbers north of Yellowstone National Park. Hunting is allowed four days per week during most of January and February.

All elk killed by hunters must be checked through a Montana Fish, Wildlife, and Parks (FWP) check station. FWP biologists collect information about elk killed, including gender, age, and pregnancy status.

Our understanding of the relationships between wolves, hunters, and elk may be bolstered by comparing data from Late Winter Study with data from the Late Hunt. Note, the time periods and durations of these events do not exactly overlap (Late Winter Study is 30 days in March, and Late Hunt is 24 days during six weeks in January and February), but comparison of the data may provide insight into elk population dynamics.

I turned to Doug Smith, Wolf Project Leader, and Tom Lemke, Montana Fish Wildlife and Parks biologist, for explanations of the respective data sets. Doug explained that, as best biologists can tell, wolves on the Northern Range kill an average of about 77 elk each March (1998-2001). Tom explained that north of Yellowstone hunters take elk during two hunting seasons: the general hunting season in the fall and the Late Hunt in January and February. Tom said that during the fall general season, hunters take about 150 to 250 elk per year (in recent years), based on a hunter harvest telephone survey. During the Late Hunt from 1996 to 2001, hunters killed from 974 to 2,465 elk per season, with an average of 1,590.

Based on their information and accumulating data, I developed a model showing hunting success by hunters and wolves (Appendix 12). This model deals only with winter killed animals, January through March. Two factors are central to the model. The first I call "pressure" and the second, "magnitude." Pressure represents the relative success (percent, not actual numbers taken) by age class, while magnitude is the actual number of elk taken.

Wolves show a greater ability to select for weaker and naive animals and have their greatest success in the calf (8 to 9 months) and older age categories (11 years and older). Hunters take naive animals and have their greatest success in the calf (7 to 8 months) age category with secondary pressure on younger animals (less than seven years old). Hunter pressure drops substantially after ten years of age, while wolf pressure increases substantially after ten years of age.

Confusion and nervousness reign among elk that were recently chased by Druid Peak wolves. The elk have just stopped running and are milling about near the wolves, which are standing over an elk they killed only minutes earlier. The dark wolf may be 253M.
DAN HARTMAN

Pressure is a relative indicator that shows the age and type of elk that wolves and hunters successfully remove from the population, while magnitude shows the real numbers taken. For the seasons of 1996 to 2001, hunters have taken an average of 1,590 elk and wolves of the Northern Range have taken an average of 77 elk (remember time frame differences). Additional wolves do exist north of Yellowstone, but are fewer in number than those studied on the Northern Range and kill fewer elk during Late Winter Study.

During the winter, wolves and hunters are most successful in taking naive elk, calves that are 7 to 9 months of age. Relative pressure by wolves on calves averages about 40 percent, while that of hunters is 18 percent. When pressure and magnitude are considered together, hunters take about 227 calves per Late Hunt and wolves take about 31 calves during Late Winter Study.

Most elk taken by hunters are from six to 18 months of age (27 percent) and progressively fewer for older age classes. Most hunters prefer prime age elk, either for food or trophies, but one-quarter take young, non-reproducing elk (about 9 percent of yearling elk are pregnant). Hunters also exert some pressure on middle-aged or prime elk.

Wolves select weak animals, mostly young and old. The average age of an adult cow elk killed by wolves is about 14 years old. By fourteen, teeth of elk are mostly worn down and these old elk, of relatively poorer nutritional status, are weaker and more susceptible to predation. Importantly, old cows are past reproductive prime and will, at best, only produce offspring a few more times, compared to a young calf which can potentially produce offspring for another 15 or so years. Targeted pressure by wolves on older cows has less impact on elk reproduction, while reducing number of animals feeding on limited forage available during the winter.

Regretfully, good information about the take by wolves is only available for the Early and Late Winter Hunts. Gathering data for non-snow months is difficult because wolves are not easily observed. Recently Global Positioning Satellite (GPS) radio collars were placed on wolves to learn more about summer kill rates but additional studies are still needed. Information gathered in the future will be particularly enlightening about the relationship of wolf populations and their interactions with wolves and hunters.

In the meantime, combined harvest by wolves and hunters of young elk affects herd size and should be carefully monitored. During some seasons, it might be necessary for hunting regulations to reduce the number of permits or limit permits to a bulls-only season.

PREDATION ON MOOSE

Moose numbers have never been high on the northern range of Yellowstone, but low numbers since wolf restoration prompted concern that wolves may be responsible for a decline. To answer this question, I turned to Dan Tyers, USDA. Forest Service biologist and the local expert on moose populations. Dan not only has conducted field research since 1985, he also has scoured all known historical reports and documents to decipher a patchy record about moose in his study area from Hellroaring Creek to Slough Creek drainages.

Dan says moose arrived in the area in late 1880s and their numbers peaked about 1945. Subsequent decreases in numbers coincided with reduced amounts of available willows. Numbers decreased sharply after the 1988 fires because of the loss of old growth lodgepole forest. Lodgepole forests provide shelter from snow and an understory of subalpine fir, the primary winter food for moose. Moose numbers were low before reintroduction and have remained low to date.

Blame for low moose numbers should not be laid solely at the feet of the wolves. Known wolf predation on northern Yellowstone moose is low, less than 10 animals. Low numbers probably reflect several reasons, including predation, continual depletion of willows by high numbers of elk, food and/or habitat loss during the 1988 fires, and recent drought conditions slowing the regeneration of willows.

PREDATION ON BISON

Formidable is an understatement when a 120-pound wolf faces a 2,000-pound bull bison. Then add the chance that this wolf has never before seen a bison, much less never been taught how to kill one by its parents. How does the wolf learn to kill the towering relic from the ice age and how long does it take to learn?

The 17 wolves brought to Yellowstone in 1996 came from an area that had both elk and bison. The Nez Perce pack, in particular, was captured while feeding on a bison. Certainly the idea had occurred to managers that bison-knowledgeable wolves placed on the west side of Yellowstone might help reduce the number of bison migrating out of the park. But, alas, this wasn't to be. Early on the wolves didn't prey on bison. The question became: Would wolves ever prey on bison, especially those wolves with no experience around bison?

Doug Smith studied forty-one wolves in Yellowstone to understand their relationship with bison. Only two of the study wolves possibly had experience with bison as pups. Through March 1999, these wolves killed only 14 bison. The bison were mostly in poor or unknown body condition with only one being in fair condition. Wolves were more successful at killing elk (21 percent of the chases) compared to killing bison (7 percent).

For the most part, killing adult bison has taken an extended period of time to develop, up to two years for some packs. Vulnerability has

Two cow bison intercept 224M as he charges towards their calves. 224M was testing for vulnerability, but the confrontational bison successfully drove him off. When bison stand their ground, wolves usually give up and move on.
DAN HARTMAN

been the key to success. Wolves killed mostly cow and calf bison. Most kills occurred in March or April, when bison were weakest. Kills were often made after bison were driven into deep snow.

Wolf strategies were simple: they directly approached bison with no attempt at concealment. When attacking, they came from the back, especially on galloping bison. Up to 14 wolves have been observed biting and hanging onto a bison at the same time.

The bison defense strategy was simple: stand your ground. When approached by wolves, 75 percent of the bison, including single bison, stood their ground. When the bison did not run, the wolves soon left. Larger herds of bison carried the stand-your-ground strategy further by grouping tightly together. Eighty-four percent of the time the wall of horns ended the standoff and the wolves left.

Some trends have portents for the future. Doug reports that bison kills increased from 1997 to 1999 and that trend continues. A couple of wolf packs, Mollie's and Nez Perce, appear to be specialists in taking bison. Bison kills for other packs have been minimal.

Mollie's pack has been able to capitalize on their experiences each winter in Pelican Valley. As fall approaches most elk migrate out of Pelican Valley, leaving mostly bison through the winter. By switching their diet to bison, Mollie's pack remains secure in its own territory.

SURPLUS KILLING AND WOUNDING

No matter what the prey species, wolves occasionally kill more animals than it appears the wolves can eat. The process is called surplus killing, and several explanations have been advanced for its occurrence.

Surplus killing may result from an innate predator response to chase anything that runs. Most of us have experienced a situation where our running triggered a domestic dog to chase after us. The same is true for wolves. The more running, the greater the excitement, and wolves may react by switching into a predation mode, killing more than one animal.

Surplus killing may also result from what in combat is referred to as the fog of battle. While a picture is often painted of coordinated strategies and movements among members of a pack, in truth, wolves often have no idea what other wolves are doing, let along coordinating movements during the intensity of an attack. During a chase, vegetation (sagebrush is often taller than a wolf), uneven landscape, and kicked up dust and especially snow often obscure the wolves' view of the prey and of other wolves. In these situations, one wolf may not know when another wolf has made a kill. Often wolves on different sides of a large herd of elk will make successful kills, and two or even three elk may be down when the "fog" clears.

Norm Bishop remembers such an incident. Norm worked for the National Park Service during the difficult years leading to the reintroduction of wolves. His position was that of interface among park personnel, scientists, managers, the public, and wolf and anti-wolf activists. As such, he served as spokesman, front man, and punching bag. To say he did his job well is an understatement. Now retired, Norm roams Lamar Valley teaching about wolves by sharing his experience and history with wolf restoration.

On February 20, 2002, Norm and others were sitting in the Yellowstone Institute classroom and listening to Dave Mech lecture on predation. Suddenly the door burst open. In strode Rick McIntyre to let the crowd know that about 150 elk and 13 wolves were just outside and it looked like the fur would fly. Teachers and students dashed for jackets, spotting scopes, and the door.

Pouring into the parking lot, watchers saw wolves in hot pursuit of elk. Cows and wolves were flying in all directions, but three subgroups were evident. In the middle of the melee stood 21M. Two groups of wolves closed on cows and one cow went down. 21M quickly galloped to the scene to deliver the coup de gras. Another cow went down, never to get up. The third group chased and tried to bring down a third cow but failed.

The groups neither knew what the others were doing or that other wolves had brought down elk. Each wolf was intent only on the chase in its corner of the playing field. Recent kills meant that the wolves were not overly hungry, but in the heat of the battle more elk were killed than the wolves could eat—surplus killing.

Another explanation for surplus killing is that it is a training process for young wolves. This theory holds that whenever the relatively rare opportunity presents itself for the young to test and hone their skills, each wolf may attempt a kill. More than one wolf may be successful.

Still another theory holds that surplus killing may provide food reserves for a later time. Wolves often return to a carcass long after a kill to feed on remains. Wolves in Lamar have been observed returning to a kill weeks later to chew on bones. Wolves also bury food underground for later use. Certainly when food is scarce, a strategy of surplus killing, especially when accompanied by caching food, is beneficial.

Finally, apparent surplus killing might result from a deficit of needed nutrients in prey. Each winter, elk become nutritionally stressed to the point they use up most of their fat and even some protein stored in muscle. In severe winters, such as the winter of 1996-1997 when hundreds of elk died, many elk may be in extremely poor nutritional condition. Meat from such elk may lack the quantity and quality of nutrients needed by wolves. Then the wolves eat the largest and best portions before quickly moving on to make another kill.

Thinking ecologically, it is apparent that no single explanation explains all situations of surplus killing. In fact, all of the above explanations, either singly or together, may explain a particular sequence of surplus killing. Ecologically, surplus killing is usually not a problem because in nature nothing will go to waste. Other scavengers from birds to coyotes to insects will thrive on remains left by wolves.

The problem comes when wolves interact with livestock. One wolf can kill, and already has killed, tens of sheep in a single night. Sheep are particularly vulnerable to surplus killing because during an attack, they run around "helter skelter" and lack a predator-escape plan. More than one domestic calf may be killed or wounded in a predation sequence. Understanding the evolutionary value of surplus killing does little to alleviate financial and psychological fears of the rancher who may have his or her life savings tied up in the herd.

Ranchers are not the only ones sensitive to surplus killing. Some hunters believe that surplus killing by wolves threatens their own hunting opportunities.

Another hunting strategy does not help the wolf image: that of wounding animals. Wolves may attack an elk and wound it before the elk drives them off or the wolves apparently give up. What appears to be a victory for the elk may simply be a great hunting strategy. If an elk is strong and in good condition, wolves should not risk injury by repeated attacks. Wounded animals seldom travel far, and wounded animals stiffen up, especially during long, cold nights. A previously unbeatable foe may now be an easier target.

Surplus killing and wounding, while helping wolves survive for tens of thousands of years, do not endear wolves to uninitiated witnesses or to those who believe their financial interests are threatened. Those supporting wolf restoration should seek innovative ways to keep wolves away from livestock, thus avoiding the potential for surplus killing and wounding.

REPRODUCTION AND GROWTH

When the season is right, territorial boundaries are marked, and the hunting is done, wolf minds turn to producing little wolves. Wolf reproductive biology differs from that of humans in many ways. Let's examine the reproductive year of wolves (Appendix 8).

BREEDING AND DENNING

The reproductive year starts around the first of December. Although most of the year females are not able to breed, they come into "heat" in December. Heat is the period during which sexual physiology gears up to produce eggs and support a pregnancy. During this period until birth of the young, the female sheds sexual hormones known as pheromones in her urine. Wolves can smell pheromones in even small quantities.

Breeding females become more aggressive, increasing their attention to territorial marking. Much of the year, alpha females often double urinate near the alpha male's scent marking locations. Females may squat during the process. But once in heat, females use more raised leg urination postures for double marking. For the female, the RLU is more of a lean forward with the hind leg extended up, out, and back. This is called by some a forward lean urination (FLU). Visual observation of body posture helps biologists identify wolves and understand their behavior.

Two pups at the Leopold den relax as two adults expand the size of the den by digging. The collared gray wolf may be 220F. Dens, or at least the den area, may be used repeatedly over several years. Most dens are on hillsides, which helps prevent flooding. DOUGLAS SMITH/NPS

In response to the alpha female's pheromones, males become attracted to her. By aggressive, dominant behavior, the alpha male keeps other potential suitors away.

The alpha female is not ready to breed until late January or early February. At that time, the female begins her estrous cycle, and drops of blood may be observed in her urine scent markings. The estrous cycle lasts about ten days. At the end of the cycle, the female sheds eggs and is receptive to mating. Interestingly, one criterion separating dogs from wolves is that dogs have two estrous cycles per year and wolves have only one.

Mating occurs near the end of estrus. A typical canine tie occurs and may last up to 30 minutes. While tied together the wolves are conspicuous and vulnerable. This compromising position must confer some benefit to the wolves. It is generally believed that the benefit comes from preventing the possible introduction of the sperm of another male until after fertilization has occurred.

Gestation lasts 60 days, plus or minus three days. About two-thirds of the way through gestation, females start exploring possible den sites and digging dens themselves. Females may dig multiple dens, as 5F did in 1995 when she dug five dens across a distance of about 12 miles. Multiple dens may confer several advantages. Den switching might occur if dens are discovered by predators, become impacted by weather such as intense cloudbursts, or become infested with parasites such as fleas. Additionally, using more than one den might help introduce new pups to a larger portion of their realm.

The den itself is usually dug on a hillside, which helps prevent flooding. Often the den is under a tree canopy, preventing direct introduction of rain or snow. Den entrances are often under and intermingled with the roots of large old trees or under rocks. This positioning may provide long-term structural integrity, allowing dens to survive from one year to the next with minimal spring

Druid Peak pack members sniff and follow the trail of intruder wolves during the 2002 breeding season. The other wolves were probably seeking mates. About 15 Druids pushed the intruders back over the ridge of Mount Norris.
TOM MURPHY

maintenance. Dens, or at least the den area, may be repeatedly used over a period of years. Perhaps a little digging each spring is all that is necessary to rejuvenate a den for another year.

Towards the end of gestation, the female "localizes," that is, she stays more and more at the den site. Other members of the pack may continue to roam, and other wolves may bring food to the female at the den site. She usually retires into her den to give birth. Following birth, the female is reproductively quiescent again until December.

Wolf watchers in the Lamar Valley have noted many variations from the stereotypic accounts of how a wolf pack interacts during breeding. The classic accounts say there is an alpha male and female that breed, while subordinates of the pack act as nursemaids, bringing home food for the pups and the mother. No other pack members breed and there is only one litter born per year per pack.

Exceptions have been noted in the past. For example, David Mech recorded multiple females breeding on Ellesmere Island, and researchers in Denali National Park have noted this event. Native peoples have also told us this in their legends. Frequent visibility of wolves in Lamar Valley has made it possible to document these exceptions, providing a more complete view wolf behavior during reproduction.

One or more packs have had two or more females successfully breeding each year since 1997. Multiple breeding has included relatively few females (14) from only three packs: Rose Creek, Druid Peak, and Chief Joseph. These females have also had relatively extended longevity within their packs. Five females, 9F, 18F, 41F, 42F, and 33F, have produced pups 5, 6, 4, 6, and 4 times, respectively (the breeding history of 42F is not completely clear). Notably, the very dominant female 40F, villainous heroine of the National Geographic film about the return of the wolves, only succeeded in producing pups 3 times.

Since standard dogma holds that only the alpha female breeds, these statistics are puzzling. The question is, why so many multiple breedings and why so frequently? Multiple breeding has allowed three packs to increase dramatically in the number of wolves. A quick review of the 2002 chart shows that most of the packs formed in Yellowstone have at least one alpha member who originated from multiple breeding packs. There definitely appears to be a selective advantage for a female to have many young to pass on her genes since few pups survive.

If maintaining the family tree appears to confer selective advantage, why do some wolf packs restrict breeding to only an alpha female? Could this be a consequence of food availability? In Yellowstone, elk have been plentiful and easy to kill. To me it makes sense to allow multiple females to breed if food is abundant. If food is a limiting factor, then breeding might be limited to the alpha female who incorporates or coerces other females to help raise the pups. It is probably significant that in the Rose Creek and Druid Peak packs, the females that bred were sisters, half-sisters (40F with 41F and 42F), daughters, or granddaughters. No non-pack females have been incorporated into these packs, assuring continuity of the bloodline and gene pool.

While one male at a time seems to retain his crown as alpha, some observations of 21M are of interest. In the summer of 2001, a large, uncollared gray male joined the Druid Peak pack. This male was observed doing RLUs while standing side-by-side with 21M and actually bred 106F. This gray male stayed with the pack through the fall of 2001. Venerable 21M was six and a half years old in the fall of 2001, an old age for a wolf. Was 21M allowing more freedom for a potential successor to his position? Or was it possible that two males doing RLUs were needed to mark the extensive territory of Druid Peak pack, which had grown to 37 wolves (observed together at one time)?

Multiple breeding has also included incestuous breeding behavior. Incestuous breeding presents the potential for inbreeding depression, the inheritance of bad genetic traits such as extra toes, or even worse. In 1997, 21M and his sister, 19F, were observed copulating and 19F gave birth to at least four pups. Alerted by a mortality mode signal (rapid beeping which occurs when a wolf does not move for four to six hours) from her radio collar, biologists found 19F dead on April 19, 1997. Her pups were found dead three days later. Necropsy revealed that other wolves had killed her, and her pups had died of starvation. Two theories about her death have been suggested, neither of which is provable.

One theory is that 19F was killed by the Druid Peak pack. The afternoon before her death, the Druid Peak pack was observed within a half mile of her den site, which was located near the border between the two packs. Druid Peak members were never observed any closer to the den or near where 19F was found dead. However, many things could have happened during the night when observers were not around.

The other theory suggests that her own pack members killed 19F because of the incestuous mating. To me, this theory is doubtful as both 8M (the alpha) and 21M were observed visiting the three widely separated dens of the Rose Creek females and bringing food to each den. Because of the distance between the dens, I believe it is unlikely that another wolf from Rose Creek came to 19F's den to kill 19F.

Certainly, a small gene pool is not the end of a wolf population. For example, all the wolves from the famous population on Isle Royale are descendants of one male and one female. However, incestuous breeding does create the possibility of reduced genetic vigor. Does nature provide mechanisms to prevent incestuous matings? Dr. Jane Packard, professor of ethology at Texas A&M University, believes so.

Jane once suggested a behavioral mechanism that tends to prevent parent/offspring inbreeding within the wolf pack. She suggests that a behavior blockage occurs during the period of socialization, essentially the first four months of the wolf's life. Simply put, if an adult, usually the father or mother, partakes in the social upbringing of a pup, they will not later breed with that pup.

As yet, there have been no cases of fathers breeding with daughters. However, one case exists of a mother, 5F, breeding with her son, 6M. Following the attack by Druid Peak pack that killed her mate (4M), 5F and 6M scraped by in 1996, going into exile in Pelican Valley. They were the only wolves in that area. In 1997, 5F did mate with her son, the only available male, and bore pups. It was incest out of necessity.

An interesting case is that of 8M. After the illegal shooting of 10M, 9F was recaptured with her eight pups and placed in the Rose Creek pen. She remained there until July 29, 1995, when a tree fell on the pen fence. Some pups escaped but remained outside the pen while 9F and the rest of the pups were inside the pen. 8M discovered the situation and started bringing food to the pups. The adoption occurred at the end of the socialization period, and 8M essentially did not socialize the pups. When 9F was released with the rest of the pups, 8M stayed with the pack as the alpha male. Not only did 8M mate with 18F, she eventually became his alpha female. Perhaps a violation of the socialization theory is the fact that in 1999 8M did breed 78F, his daughter who he had also socialized.

While not incestuous, it is interesting to note that two males have breed with sisters. 21M mated with 40F and 42F, and 34M mated with 16F and 17F.

MATE THEFT

At times, territorial intrusions may not be over disputed boundaries but rather raids seeking mates. For a young or widowed male, the apparent need to have his own pack is high, prompting forays into territories of existing packs. The forays have resulted in deaths, but some males, such as 21M, are lucky enough to find a pack where they become the new alpha male. Other males simply find a female and leave.

It was about December 24, 2001, when Bob Landis and other watchers were sitting near the confluence of Soda Butte Creek and Lamar River watching an elk calf that had been wounded by wolves

The stare of a wild wolf is intense and piercing. Like the summer flower, the bright eyes of this Druid Peak wolf say "forget-me-not." DONALD M. JONES

the day before. They also saw the gray male, 113M from the Chief Joseph pack, deep in Druid Peak territory near the river confluence. The distance separating 113M from the Druid Peak pack was only 100 yards.

About the same time the watchers saw 113M, so did the Druid Peak pack, and a chase ensued. The pack chased 113M to near the confluence where 113M lost them. Bob said he thought it was over, but soon 113M again approached the Druid Peak pack. The second chase started and came close to the wounded elk calf, which spooked and ran into the river seeking shelter. The pack was distracted and investigated the calf. Although the river was shallow and not much of a barrier, the wolves chose not to go after the calf.

At the time, the Druid Peak pack was large with close to 30 members, many of whom were yearlings. After investigating the calf, the pack lost interest and started leaving. Five or six yearlings went to 113M to check him out. The scene was very similar to that when 21M was accepted into the Druid Peak pack. The yearlings swarmed around 113M, sniffing him, while 113M stood tall and still. There was a lot of tail wagging.

While the social testing was going on, 21M was about 200 yards away. After about 15 minutes, 21M came over and chased away 113M on his own. Bob said, "It was as if other pack members could not understand why 21M was chasing away a potential new friend."

Interactions continued off and on between 113M and the Druid Peak pack for about three weeks. It became apparent that 113M was trying to attract a female, not join the pack. Some yearling females may have actually left the pack and traveled with 113M for a time.

In time 113M seemed to settle down around the Tower area but occasionally was observed back in Lamar near the Druid Peak pack. In June, it became apparent that one of the yearling females, now two years old, had given birth. Her den was located a couple of miles from the main Druid Peak pack den. 21M occasionally visited the den, but so did 113M. 113M managed to never be around when 21M showed up. Interestingly, members of the Druid Peak pack brought food to their sister, thereby helping to raise the pups of a male, 113M, from another pack.

The 113M event is reminiscent of the way 34M of the Chief Joseph pack acquired his two female partners back in 1997. After a car killed his alpha female 32F in the summer of 1996, 34M started mate hunting. After some raids into Druid Peak territory where 34M was attacked by the Druid Peak pack, he succeeded in luring away yearlings 16F and 17F. Over time, the females were again seen with their birth pack but returned to be with 34M. Matings occurred between 34M and both females. However, each female maintained her own den and 34M visited both dens.

Mate theft appears to occur over the period of weeks and is not merely the result of a single foray. Young wolves, yearlings and pups, are the first to approach and accept intruders into their territory.

PHYSICAL GROWTH

In April, female wolves give birth in the den to an average of six pups. Pups grow and develop rapidly (Appendix 9). They weigh less than a pound at birth and their eyes and ears are closed. Their eyes open at about two weeks while the pups are still deep in the den. Ear canals open at about 20 days. From two to three weeks of age, pups emerge from their den, and they weigh about seven pounds. They are already play fighting to establish their positions in the social dominance hierarchy of the pack. Newly opened ears allow them to hear their first feeble attempts at barking and howling.

By five weeks they have grown to 13 pounds and their mother is weaning them. Pups gallop behind their parents for short distances and gain the ability to travel. Once they are able to travel, they will be taken to a rendezvous site. The rendezvous site is usually a prominent open area where pack members socialize and howl together. The trip to the rendezvous occurs at about eight to ten weeks. By this age, males are becoming heavier than females. The size difference is obvious. Females may be as small as 15 pounds and males as heavy as 22 pounds

Around 20 weeks the pups start getting their permanent teeth and develop their first coat of winter fur. They will need heavy fur for Yellowstone's cold. Around 30 weeks, the pups start to travel with the rest of the pack during short hunting forays. Males may reach 80 pounds.

Growth is very rapid through at least the first nine months of a wolf's life. Females grow at a slower rate than males. Based on weights obtained while Yellowstone wolves were being handled, by nine months of age males average 95 pounds and females average 83 pounds.

At the end of a year the pups have reached maximum skeletal growth. The growth sections of the bones grow together or close. There can only be small amounts of bone growth after this, but the animals may continue to increase muscle size and body mass. Large males may be 95 pounds at the end of a year, but small females may be only 60 pounds.

Growth rates slow after nine to 12 months of age, but growth may continue for the rest of the wolf's life. Average growth curves for male and female wolves are shown in Appendix 10. For Yellowstone adult wolves (judged to be 24 months or older), the average weight of males is 110 pounds and the average weight of females is 94 pounds. There does appear to be a decrease in weight of older male wolves.

Many wolf watchers want to know which wolf is the biggest and what their favorite wolf weighs. Appendix 11 shows individual weights. The heaviest male wolves to date were 6M (141 pounds) and 28M (140 pounds). The heaviest female wolves

to date were 5F (116 pounds) and 27F (115 pounds). Remember though, a wolf can gain 10 or more pounds at one meal and a day or so later have lost all that weight. When researchers capture a wolf, there is no way to know how much food may be in the wolf's stomach.

SOCIAL DEVELOPMENT

Physical growth goes hand-in-hand with sociological development. Behaviorists define two phases of growth: socialization and juvenile. From birth to mid-August, pups go through the socialization phase where they learn to be socially responsible members of the pack. From mid-August to the end of the year, pups go through a juvenile phase where they begin to learn to be functional hunting members of the pack.

Wolf pups must build emotional bonds with pack members to assure pack continuity. To form bonds, wolves wrestle, play, and howl together. Social movements of running, climbing, jumping, and playing facilitate learning to hunt as a pack. Playing also develops muscles and coordination necessary for survival.

Developing and understanding social position in the pack is key. Within a month of birth, pups are initiating dominance relationships to test who is higher or lower on the social ladder. They play, snarl, growl, grimace, threaten, bite, and fight. These mock battles and face-offs establish leaders and followers, but most importantly they establish future alphas or dominants.

Critical diet changes occur early because pups must switch from mother's milk to meat. Adults eat food at a kill site and return to the rendezvous site, where they are greeted with joyous exuberance. Pups that lick the faces of returning members may be rewarded by regurgitated food, an action that furthers bonding. Eventually the adults bring home pieces of non-digested meat.

For adult wolves, teaching pups can be as trying process, according to Jason Wilson, wolf watcher. Jason and his wife, Deb Lineweaver, hail from Virginia. The couple started observing wildlife in Lamar Valley about two decades before the wolves came. According to Jason, it was a July day when adults from the Druid Peak pack led their pups to the rendezvous site for the first time. The wolves were strung out in a long line with several adults leading, pups in the middle, and an adult at the end. The pups were going as fast as their short, little legs and inquisitive minds would allow; they paused to look at everything.

(Left) Pups from the Swan Lake pack adorn their den entrance. Pups emerge from their den at about 14 to 21 days of age. They stay at the den until they are eight to ten weeks old, when the pack moves to a rendezvous site. The size of the dirt apron testifies to the magnitude of the den's tunnels and chambers below ground. DOUGLAS SMITH/NPS

(Far left) The raised tail displays an adult's alpha status to the pups of the Swan Lake pack, who submissively greet their returning parents. The parents were just returning from killing a large bull elk and their stomachs were full of food to regurgitate to the pups. JESS R. LEE

A young wolf pauses along a river. By mid-summer, pups are large enough to follow their parents and move to a rendezvous site. This site is usually a prominent open area where pack members socialize and howl together. Learning to hunt comes next. BOB SCHILLEREFF

Climbing a small knoll, the wolves surveyed the surrounding area. There was a herd of about 50 bison with 10 to 12 bulls pawing and bellowing. Bull bison, feeling an early rush of pre-breeding testosterone, were head butting and creating quite a stir of dust. It was a formidable arena. The pups took one look and spooked, turning tail and galloping back the way they had just come. Soon the pups dropped down out of sight into the river channel.

The adults lay down to wait. It was a long wait, more than an hour. Eventually, an adult, 42F, got up and went back, disappearing from sight. Another long wait. Nothing. Another adult got up and went back. Nothing. Finally, all the adults got up and went back. Another long wait ensued.

Eventually they all appeared again in a long line headed for the knoll. Pups hung back, but the adults all went to the top of the knoll that overlooked the bison herd. The adults then proceeded down among the bison, which mostly ignored them. There the wolves lay down.

Eventually the boldest pup came to the closest adult, who was at the edge of the herd. The adult got up and greeted the pup. The adult then walked with the pup to the next closest adult, who got up and greeted it. The second adult then led the pup through the herd to the next adult and so on. Another pup came forward to be met and escorted through the bison herd. Eventually all the pups came and were escorted through the bison herd. Armed with their new knowledge, the pups didn't so much as look back as the pack all got up and wandered on to the rendezvous site.

As pups grow to adulthood, it is a continual learning process. As they reach sexual maturity at about 22 months of age, some will chose to leave the pack, perhaps to start their own packs. Male wolves may disperse as far as 500 miles. Females usually do not go as far. Some young wolves will remain with the pack to help with future litters. Their loyalty to the alpha pair insures that genes of the parents, which they also carry, will be passed on to future generations.

The growing up process is dangerous. The average life span for a wolf is about six months. Six months may seem like a short life span, but it is because of heavy mortality on wolf pups during their first year. Larger animals, including bears, coyotes, cougars, elk, and birds of prey, may kill pups. Cliffs, diseases, starvation, flood water and river crossings all take their toll.

LEARNING TO HUNT

The juvenile learning phase, which lasts until the wolf is about two years old, prepares pups to be predators. Wolves must learn to be successful hunters. Those that don't, don't live long.

Once pups have tasted regurgitated meat, they must learn to eat solid meat brought home by returning adults. Next, pups have to associate eating meat with killing. First, pups play/practice on dead mice captured by adults. Next, adult wolves may bring home wounded prey such as mice, squirrels, or rabbits. Pups initially play with these animals, but when they die they are eaten. Finally, pups learn to kill their play toys to speed up access to their meal.

Once pups have learned to kill, they are ready for a real but playful hunt. Playing imitates killing behavior. Pups start limited mouse hunting to hone skills of stalking, chasing, and pouncing.

Finally the day comes when the pups join the adults on their first hunt. Perhaps it will only be a rabbit not far from home, but the pups must learn when, where, and how to hunt. They must learn when to be quiet, how to stalk silently, when to test herds for weak members, how to recognize weak members, when to chase, and how to kill. It takes time to learn these steps and many hunts fail. Young wolves would often go hungry if it were not for skilled parents. However, even with parents, the wolves may attempt 20 chases before they make a kill.

Ward Hughson, a Canadian wolf field technician, shared his observations and theories about the "first hunt." Imagine the pups timidly following mom and dad. They crest the ridge and, there, close in front, is an elk. The pup weighs 50 pounds but the bull elk

Three members of the Druid Peak pack were chasing 113M from the Chief Joseph pack and several Druid females (not in photo) up the ridge of Mount Norris during the 2002 breeding season. Apparently 113M had entered Druid territory and lured away the female wolves. The two groups never came within a quarter of a mile of each other.
TOM MURPHY

weighs 600 pounds. The pups quickly slink away, unwilling to go ahead. So their parents take them back to the rendezvous site and give them more training.

Next time out, the pups are primed. They are ready to go. They are invincible teenagers. The pack crests a ridge and sees an elk. The pups scratch the ground with great ferocity and turn to Dad, barking "Let's go." The elk looks up at the noise and runs away.

Dad plows into the pups. In wolf talk, Ward says, he lets them know that they follow his lead. Pups do not run ahead. They don't make a noise. Pups don't do anything until Dad has done it first. More lessons follow. Maybe on the next hunt they get an elk. Rick McIntyre fondly remembers one learning-to-hunt event during the summer of 1995 in Lamar Valley. As Rick looked across the valley, he spotted 8M not doing much of anything. The wolf was barely a yearling, full of curiosity and on a learning spree.

As Rick watched, 8M suddenly fixed his gaze on something. Next, 8M dropped into a stalking posture and started moving forward. Rick quickly scanned the direction that 8M was going, but he could not spot any reasonable prey. All Rick saw was a big bull bison, "maybe 1,500 pounds."

With great stealth, 8M moved forward, successfully stalking the bison to within two feet of its rear end. The bison was facing the other direction and unaware of pending doom. Then the situation became funny. The wolf stood erect to its full height, vacating his stalking posture, no more stealth. But what to do? 8M looked confused. He had stalked the bison but didn't know what to do next. He just stood there.

Perhaps the bison smelled 8M or 8M made a noise, but the bison slowly swung his head rearward to look at 8M. The bison's huge eyes seemed unimpressed, and he turned his head back and resumed chewing his cud. Soon a fly or something bothered the bull and he

flicked his tail. This was too much for 8M! The young wolf turned tail and ran away.

Instinctively or from playing as a pup, 8M had known how to stalk but did not know the rest of what to do. Later 8M became the alpha male of Rose Creek Pack and has been involved with hundreds of successful hunts and kills.

Nathan Varley, a young lad experienced to the gills with Yellowstone wildlife, has been fascinated with the hunting learning process. He shared his observations made in Little America of lower Lamar Valley during March 1997. The winter just ending had been one of the harshest on record, with thousands of elk dying.

It was about dark as Nathan watched the Rose Creek pups; there were no adult wolves around. Nathan and the wolves spotted an elk calf. The calf was in bad shape. It stumbled through the snow with a blank stare. Nathan remembers thinking, "Here's an easy kill."

The pups came on the attack. They darted at the calf, then jumped back. Their behavior was very timid. If the calf flinched or stumbled, the wolves jumped away. Action migrated down the slope towards a bison herd. Bison spooked the pups away, and the calf survived that day. Something was missing from the pups. Although hungry, none was ready to make the kill. They had yet to learn to make that last killing lunge.

Sometimes learning to hunt can be a matter of necessity with little time for experimenting. Deb Guernsey remembers an April day in 1996 when she sat on a knoll we call South Butte, just southeast of the Children's Fire Trail. By April, 7F had already whelped, leaving her mate, 2M, without a hunting partner. 2M had to provide for 7F and their new pups.

Deb watched 2M approach a herd of 30 to 40 cow elk and start a chase. He singled out one cow that was much slower than the rest of the herd. The cow turned and faced 2M. For a brief moment there was a standoff, and then he attacked. With all his might, 2M charged in and seized the cow by her throat. Holding the elk in his death grip, 2M suffocated her. Necessity had been the mother of learning. 2M figured out a way to kill by himself and he became good at it.

DISEASES AND OTHER DANGERS

Wolves are susceptible to all diseases that affect dogs, according to Mark Johnson, a professional wildlife veterinarian. Mark was instrumental in designing health care for wolves from the time they were captured in Canada until they were at home in Yellowstone. He says some diseases can be individually fatal but usually don't limit the overall population.

One disease of concern is canine parvovirus, an infectious viral disease. Parvovirus can move through a population of coyotes or wolves like a cold or flu moves through the human population. Parvo, as it is called, is carried by domestic dogs. The dogs themselves may not show symptoms and are potential sources of new and more virulent strains. Visitors to Yellowstone with dogs should keep them close to roads. It is required that visitors clean up their dogs' defecation.

Evening light reveals a Nez Perce wolf crossing Nez Perce Creek to begin a night hunt. Wild wolves face numerous dangers, including river crossings, injuries from hunting, fights with other wolves, and disease. Only about 20 percent of wild wolves live to two years of age. JESS R. LEE

Parvovirus is known to exist in Yellowstone coyotes, and antibodies reveal exposure to parvo in Yellowstone wolves. Adult coyotes and wolves may survive parvovirus attacks, but young pups are especially vulnerable. Parvo infections seem to surge when temperatures are hot during the summer. Unexplained summer losses of wolf pups in Yellowstone hint at possible parvovirus infections, but it has yet to be documented.

In the wild, only about 20 percent of wolves live to two years of age. For wolves that reach two years of age, the life expectancy is about five years and some live to ten years of age. A ten-year-old wolf is very old and unusual. In Yellowstone, the longest-lived wolves are probably 2M, 18F, 21M, and 42F. When 2M died in 2002, he was eight or more years old. Wolves 18F and 21M are the only wolves born in 1995 that are still alive. In 2003, they will be eight years old. 42F was probably born in 1994 and is now about nine years old, a grand old matriarch.

It is instructive to consider known sources of mortality in the Yellowstone wolves. Of 126 known adult deaths in the Yellowstone ecosystem, the leading cause of mortality is management removal for livestock depredations. This has accounted for 40 percent (49) of the losses. Natural deaths account for 29 percent (36). Natural deaths include one wolf scalded to death in a thermal feature, six killed while hunting, 16 killed in interpack territorial conflicts, one killed by conflict within its own pack, two killed in an avalanche, four drowned, one killed by a mountain lion, one impaled on a stick, and 19 deaths of unknown causes. Interestingly, only three wolves appear to have died of old age. Twelve wolves (10 percent) have been killed by vehicles, nine (7 percent) illegally shot, three (2 percent) collateral loss during coyote control, and one (1 percent) illegally poisoned. At least another 63 wolves, including over 53 pups, are unaccounted for.

The loss of 12 wolves from being hit by vehicles points out the danger of crossing highways. Most of these accidents have occurred in the northwest corner of Yellowstone National Park along Highway 191 where the speed limit is 55 mile per hour. The 45-mph speed limit in the rest of the park has undoubtedly prevented additional wolf losses.

THE FUR COAT

A wolf in its prime of life is a magnificent creature. Its fur coat catches the eye of even casual wolf watchers. The coat is thick and lush. The fur coat is comprised of a layer of underfur and a layer of guard hairs. Underfur consists of short, very thin hairs, while guard hairs are long and thick. Guard hairs protect the rest of the coat, while underfur provides insulation. Three overlapping layers of guard hairs, called capes, start over the shoulder and extend back to the rump, providing not only protection but also water resistance.

Fur varies both seasonally and over the life of a given wolf. Each spring, wolves shed their winter coat. During the shedding process, they look decrepit and give the impression of an unhealthy animal. Quite the opposite, shedding allows the wolf to be cooler in the summer and sets the stage for new hair growth before winter. Summer coats are short while winter coats have guard hairs more than three inches long and underfur more than two inches long. Fur is at its densest at the peak of winter (December and January) and begins to thin out as spring approaches. Hairs actually break off and ends split. As wolves age, their hair becomes lighter in color, turning gray and white. There may be some loss of hair density with age.

Guard hairs are banded with stripes of gray, brown, black, or white. Underfur tends to be all one color. Coat color may reflect combinations of guard hair and underfur. For example, a light brown underfur with mostly gray guard hairs may appear reddish, a color category called tawny. In general, guard hairs provide the dominant color and little of the underfur shows through.

Six coat colors have been observed in Yellowstone wolves: gray, black, silver-black, blue, red, and white. Coat colors are determined by several interacting factors including genetics and age. Most wolves across North America are gray, often more than 90 percent of a given population. Black is rare except in the Canadian Rockies and now in Yellowstone. Black wolves have, on an annual average, made up 46 percent of the Yellowstone population, an unusually high proportion. Wolf 13M, the Gray Ghost as he was known, was blue/gray in color, a gun-metal gray that glinted blue in the sun.

Many Yellowstone wolves start turning silver-black to gray at an early age. For example, 9F and her daughters 40F, 41F, and 42F were distinctly black when young. By three years of age, they had silver on their backs, flanks, and muzzle. By six to seven years of age, they were almost completely silver-black, starting to turn white. This rapid graying is a genetic trait and differs markedly from the slow infusion of white hairs that occurs normally with age. With age, white hairs appear in the coat of wolves, especially on the muzzle and back. The change to white is evident in 21M and 42F, both of whom have become silver-white with only little black showing.

The proportion of white wolves increases to the north, rarely exceeding eight percent of a population until the Arctic, where every wolf may be white. Only one white wolf was brought to Yellowstone, 39F, the original alpha female of the Druid Peak pack.

(Left) Long, thick guard hairs cover dense, short underfur on this young gray wolf from the Druid Peak pack. Guard hairs generally create the fur color and protect the underfur, which provides insulation. Fur is most dense in January and February. DR. JIM MCGRAW

(Right) Most of the Druid Peak pack was farther up the Lamar River towards Cache Creek when a Druid Peak member (possibly 103F) came to this ridgetop and howled to the pack. For a long time they howled back and forth, delighting wolf watchers. PETE BENGEYFIELD

BEHAVIOR WITHIN THE PACK

Behavior can be classified into intraspecific behavior, occurring among individuals of one species, and interspecific behavior, occurring between different species. Interspecific behavior will be covered in the section about ecology. Here we will cover behavior within wolf packs.

ALPHA ROLES

The glue that holds a pack together consists of the alpha male and alpha female. The roles of alphas and their continuity of leadership are pivotal to pack longevity. Packs tend to occupy a territory for many years, often continuing the main gene pool during that time.

Maintenance of leadership may be subtle. When Soda Butte pack was brought from Canada, 13M (weight 113 pounds) was believed to be the alpha male. His presence, however, was not prominent and certainly not bold. Whenever the pack was observed, 13M either was not seen or only glimpsed in the forest. This behavior earned him the name of Gray Ghost. In late 1995 a young male, 12M (weight 122 pounds) became prominent in the pack and appeared to be taking over the alpha status. However, after December 21, 1995, 12M was no longer observed with the pack. The old veteran, 13M, had exerted his dominance, and after that 12M traveled separately from the pack.

When the Soda Butte pack was recaptured northeast of the park and moved into the park, 13M was examined. Analysis showed he

The Druid Peak pack begins a hunting trip by traveling single file up a low ridge on Mount Norris. In Yellowstone, biologists note that alpha wolves do not always lead the pack when traveling. Other wolves sometimes take the lead.
MICHAEL H. FRANCIS

had a healed broken leg. During his recovery from this serious injury, the pack must have provided him with food. Pack membership and perhaps alpha status do confer benefits.

The breeding or alpha pair is key to reproductive success and pack continuity. Loss of one of the pair might be devastating and, prior to restoration, little was known about the formation of a new breeding pair after the loss of one member. But that changed in December 1997.

In late November, the Druid Peak pack ventured east of the park where alpha male 38M and beta male 31M were shot and killed. On December 4, 1997, the remaining members of the Druid Peak pack returned to the Lamar Valley. The pack consisted of seven members: alpha female 40F, beta female 42F, and five pups.

At the same time, 21M was two-and-a-half years old and dispersing from his Rose Creek pack. In his formative years, territorial conflict with the Druid Peak pack had resulted in the death of two of his siblings. On December 3, 21M was seen traveling alone along the border of the Druid Peak territory, howling frequently. Being caught in the territory of another pack often results in death for the intruder.

Bob Landis documented the following event on film. Early on the morning of December 8, the Druid Peak pack was traveling but stopping frequently to howl. At 9:47 a.m., 21M was seen with 39F, a former alpha female of the Druid Peak pack, after they left a deer kill. 39F was the mother of Druid Peak members 40F, 41F, and 42F but she had been ostracized from the pack. She and 21M split up and 39F was not seen again that day.

At 11:17, the Druid Peak pack was seen watching 21M about 500 yards away. 40F and 42F began to chase him at full speed. Eventually 21M stopped and faced the whole pack, which had already stopped. Pack members howled for 45 minutes and then 21M began to growl, bark, and howl while wagging his tail from side to side. The pack left, and 21M followed at a distance.

The first approach was by pup 106F. She used several play-bows and went into a submissive posture. 21M held what has been called a "presentation posture" characterized by "erect and outward-pointed ears, head held high, tail elevated and wagging, and a stiff-legged stance." Next, 21M did two RLUs, the first record of 21M ever doing this dominant behavior.

To make a long story short, over the next several hours 40F first accepted 21M and then so did 42F. During the process, both females used behaviors including averted eyes, play-bows, and anal sniffing. Tail wagging and presentation posture were most common for 21M. Finally, the whole pack accepted 21M by gathering around him. The pack moved out of sight, and radio signals at 4:30 p.m. indicated that 21M was traveling with the pack. He became the new alpha male.

While we will never know for sure how the wolves communicated their intentions, several modes were probably used: vocalization, pursuit and flight, and ritualized posturing. While initial howls probably represented territorial advertisement, they may have communicated the lack of an alpha male in the pack. Pursuit and flight allowed the wolves to evaluate each other's intentions. The initial pursuit did not seem to display territorial aggression. Play behaviors by the adults conveyed dominance positions and evaluated strengths. The presentation posture of 21M communicated confidence and dominance. At one point, 21M hung his chin over the back of 42F and placed a paw on her back. Anal sniffing may have allowed communication of reproductive information and increase familiarity. In general, behaviors were used in a non-threatening manner.

This remarkable sequence did much to advance our knowledge of wild wolves. The rapidity with which 21M joined a new pack and become the alpha male was dramatic.

The probability of a wolf leaving its birth pack and becoming an alpha of another pack is low. Simply being away from a pack reduces survivorship potential. The additional risk of moving into another

Alpha 21M (third from the left) and several pups from the Druid Peak pack howl at the approach of 42F (out of picture), 21M's mate and the pups' mother. Howling serves for communication, location, and social bonding. Howling also advertises territories and perhaps relays information about pack composition. DAN HARTMAN

pack territory is immense. Then, to find a pack where the alpha male is missing is very unusual. Of note, we have not observed an outside male wolf displace a current alpha male of pack leadership.

THE STRESS OF ALPHA STATUS

"When thinking about alpha status, some might consider it the ultimate position, the top dog, so to speak," explains researcher Jennifer Sands. Certainly, there appear to be benefits to being the only wolf that breeds and a definite down side to being a subordinate, who is the target of aggression from those higher on the dominance hierarchy. But are there hidden physiological costs to dominance? To answer that question, Jennifer devised a three-year study looking at alpha status. Hers was a complex project linking social status, aggression, and reproductive success.

First Jennifer had to define social status by ranking animals according to outcomes of interactions. She watched encounters as subtle as approaching each other, ear position, tail position, where wolves slept, and how close they slept to each other. For each encounter, she scored a "winner" and ranked the wolves in a pack from alpha on down the social hierarchy.

Next, Jennifer took her cue from captive breeders of wolves, who suggested that lower-ranking animals were socially stressed. Other stress might be caused by lack of food, harsh weather, and dangerous encounters. From an evolutionary perspective, if social stress is high or long lasting, other body components such as the immune system, reproductive system, brain function, or longevity might be affected, perhaps reducing a wolf's ability to pass on its genes or genetic heritage.

All Jennifer needed was a measure of stress, which she found in stress hormones. Stress hormones chemically are known as glucocorticoids, and they are secreted in scat. It was tedious work to

On Valentine's Day 2002, 21M diligently follows his mate, 42F, up Junction Butte. During the breeding season, males often follow females, checking and affirming their reproductive status. A study in Yellowstone appears to show that alpha animals have higher levels of stress than other pack members. Perhaps there are physiological "costs" associated with alpha status. DAN HARTMAN

observe wolves defecating and then, later, find that very scat. Nonetheless, Jennifer persevered and collected 351 scat, including 117 from known individuals. Back in the lab, the scat yielded up their hormonal treasure and blew away conventional theory.

Yes, stress hormones were elevated, but not in the subordinates. Alpha animals showed higher levels of stress hormones. The study generated more questions than it answered. Why should dominance create stress? Dominant animals did not engage in social interactions any more than other wolves, but they do win more often. Winning shouldn't be stressful.

Presence of stress hormones in dominant animals suggests there may be a cost to "alphaship." Further studies are needed to determine what that cost is. The take-home message is that social stress does not appear to place a hormonal limitation on subordinate reproduction.

ALPHA FEMALES

There are two sides to the alpha status for a female. First, she must produce offspring and second she must control reproduction of other females. When the alpha female of the pack fails to produce her own offspring, she may be ousted from her alpha role and even lose her position in the pack. Two notable examples of this occurred in Yellowstone. Female 39F was the alpha female in 1996 when the pack arrived from Canada. She was mother of 40F, 41F, and 42F. Biologists introduced 39F and 38M in the acclimation pen in Yellowstone. 38M was from a different pack in Canada.

Although 39F and 38M were placed together in time for mating in 1996, they failed to produce a litter. Perhaps failure was due to the stress of translocation or perhaps 39F was at the end of her reproductive success, or some of both.

By fall of 1996, 40F was taking over the alpha position and aggressively shoving her mother out. Her mother traveled alone and

was not located for periods of time. After the females bred in the spring of 1997, 39F returned to the pack. Only 41F and 42F had pups that year. Female 39F served as a nursemaid for the pups that season and was often alone at the den with the pups. Still, 40F solidified her position by again ousting 39F in the fall.

40F's aggressive behavior soon also drove 41F from the pack. Maggie Purvis remembers the day 41F was driven off. We were by Soda Butte when Maggie saw 41F settle down with head, neck, and part of her chest in view and begin a long mournful howl. Maggie remembers other howls from the hills on the south side of the road. Maggie felt that the Druid Peak pack, mostly hidden, seemed to be saying, "Don't come back." Maggie said it was incredible to watch a wolf howl, but the message left her empty-hearted. 41F never returned to the Druid Peak pack.

Female 39F was around the pack in the winter of 1997-1998 but could never regain a position with the pack. Male 21M took over as alpha in December of 1997 and 40F bore his young in the spring of 1998. On March 4, 1998, 39F was illegally shot outside the park.

39F was white when she arrived, the only white wolf to come to Yellowstone. She was an old wolf with daughters of perhaps two different years. Her age and lack of breeding allowed her daughter to eventually oust her from the pack, even though she later served to help care for pups.

Here is a last, highly speculative thought on 39F. What was her role on the morning of December 8, 1997, when she was with 21M before he encountered the Druid Peak pack? Did she play a role in communicating to 21M that there was no alpha male with the pack? Might her scent on 21M have helped in the introduction process? Did 39F help her pack one last time? These are questions that will never be answered, but stating them brings some solace to bereaved wolf watchers.

Contrary to the authoritarian role of 40F in the Druid Peak pack, 9F of the Rose Creek pack was called the benevolent mother, a human concept of course. While she was alpha, 9F allowed other pack females to breed in 1997, 1998, and 1999. She did not seem to exert aggressive dominance over her subordinates.

While maintaining alpha status may be rough as with 40F or tolerant as with 9F, older female breeders do seem to lose their position within the pack, sometimes violently. In early 1998 21M was observed mating with 40F and 42F (42F had probably borne pups in 1997). That spring 40F stayed at the traditional Druid Peak den north of Lamar trailhead, and 42F denned north of the road, close to the Lamar field station but just out of sight. During this time 42F was often at this site and seldom traveled with the pack.

One day in May, 40F came to the den of 42F and a fierce fight ensued. Wolf watchers on the road could hear the wolves fighting but couldn't see what was happening. From that day on, 42F never returned to her den. She was eventually seen traveling with the pack. Biologists located the den but could find no evidence of pups. However, they were not able to reach the end of the den tunnel.

It is possible that 42F was undergoing a false pregnancy for which wolves are known. It is my opinion that 42F had pups and that 40F killed them. Evidence may have remained deep in the tunnel or may have been removed by scavengers before biologists visited the site.

Again in 1999, 40F, 42F, and 106F were observed mating with 21M. The six and only pups seen in 1999 were at the traditional den site occupied by 40F. Did 42F become pregnant? Could 40F

With tails wagging and other body language, the Druids communicate with each other as they begin traveling, probably on a hunting expedition.
MARK MILLER

have killed pups of 42F again or might some of the six pups have been 42F? We will never know because all pups eventually died.

In 2000, 42F, 103F, and 105F had a den site south of the Lamar River several miles from the traditional den site occupied by 40F. Just before dark on Saturday, May 6, 2000, 40F was observed near 42F's den, dominating the three females. Then night fell. The next day 40F was found, injured and bleeding badly, in a culvert under the road just east of the Lamar field station.

Initially suspecting that 40F had been hit by a car, a non-natural event, the decision was made to try to help her. Shock had set in, and 40F did not even need to be sedated. She was gently placed in the warm cab of a truck, where she later died.

Biologists and wolf watchers soon realized that 40F had been badly mauled, apparently by other wolves. A speculative scenario is that 40F followed the three females to their den and attacked their pups. As 40F attacked the pups, motherhood overcame subordinate behavior and one or more of the other females attacked 40F.

This scenario is supported by the fact at least six pups had been seen at 42F's den, but later, 42F was observed moving only four pups. It is possible that 42F moved other pups at night, but it is doubtful.

The dominance mechanism of killing pups, especially year after year, may have failed for 40F. For females, it appears that maintaining alpha and breeding status is difficult and occurs only on a short-term basis. Alpha females have left their packs to die alone or disappear. No alpha female has died of old age while with her pack.

Number 40F was a strong alpha with a reputation for business. She was aggressive, stern, and rigid. Perhaps more than other wolves, she liked to chase and kill coyotes, disposing them from her territory. 40F would be missed, if not by the wolves at least by the wolf watchers.

Three days after 40F died, 42F regrouped the pack. With relief, wolf watchers realized the wolves were going to take care of the next generation of young.

SHARED LEADERSHIP

David Mech, Rolf Peterson, and Doug Smith have questioned the popular perception that leadership equates with breeding status, believing that leadership is not exactly the same as breeding status. In other words, any wolf in the dominance hierarchy (dominant, breeding, breeding subordinate females, or non-breeders) may lead the pack at various times, in various circumstances.

Based on this idea, Amy Jacobs, a student of Rolf Peterson, studied leadership in Yellowstone. Amy, Rolf, Dave, Doug, and Tom Drummer looked at several behavioral indicators of leadership, including leading the pack while traveling or hunting and the initiation of pack behavior. They considered activity initiation occurred when one wolf prompted the following: arousing the pack from rest, traveling after group rallies (greeting ceremonies), chasing prey, changing directions during travel or defending the pack from trespassing wolves.

The team found that individual, pack, and even seasonal variations exist in leadership and initiation patterns. While breeding wolves led the pack about 78 percent of the time, it was not all the time. Leading was equally divided between the breeding female and male. Breeding wolves initiated activities about 75 percent of the time.

The team stresses that the idea of leadership only by a dominant alpha male is erroneous. The usual pattern is for the high-ranking male and female wolf, typically the primary breeding pair, to provide most leadership. Pack responsibilities and leadership are shared by the pair and even with other pack members. Subordinate wolves sometimes provide leadership during travel. Individual roles of shared leadership may exist seasonally, such as during the pup-rearing season

(Left) One of the park's best-known alpha wolves, 21M of the Druid Peak pack pauses before returning to a kill in April 2002. The pack had killed an elk close to the road, but other pack members left when people arrived at dawn. 21M and 224M, braver than other pack members, returned to feed despite the presence of people. The appearance of silver hairs in 21M's black coat indicates advancing age. He was seven years old in this photograph. CHRISTOPHER BLY

(Right) Trailing—walking in the footprints made by lead wolves—saves energy for Mollie's Pack in the deep snow of Pelican Valley. DOUGLAS SMITH/NPS

when males concentrate on travel and hunting and females focus on rearing pups. Certainly, switching leadership has obvious energetic benefits when breaking trail through deep, soft snow.

The team dislikes the term alpha wolf. Dave Mech argues that the dominance hierarchy of the typical single-breeding-pair pack merely represents parent-offspring dominance. The team explains that "as short-hand for 'dominant breeder,' 'alpha' does seem to be appropriate for packs of multiple breeders." But they believe "alpha" falsely implies a hierarchical system with a linear "pecking order."

Incipient leadership occurs in subordinate males prior to dispersal and in subordinate breeding females. With females, incipient leadership may smooth the transition from one dominant breeding female to the next. Since subordinate breeding females are often daughters, this type of transition may improve survival of the female gene pool.

SUBORDINATE WOLVES

The role of subordinates is critical to pack survival. In general, yearling and older non-breeding wolves may serve the pack by finding food and assisting with chases and kills. Their most important services may be babysitting and bringing food to pups of the year.

The value of the young wolf is individual and may change with maturity. Yearling wolves seem to play a role in attending the den, but their attendance is haphazard with no specific pattern. Yearlings are neither large enough nor skilled enough to be of regular help with hunting. The presence of yearlings at the den does provide extra sentries to sound the alarm at approaching danger. Their anti-intruder behavior contributes to pup survivorship.

Linda Thurston, one of the longest running, most dedicated researchers in the Wolf Project, studied the role of subordinates for a master's thesis. During her thesis research, she recorded all the comings and goings and behavioral interactions at the social hub of wolf existence, the den, from dawn to dusk.

Linda has observed an indirect benefit of yearlings. About four weeks after the birth of their pups, breeding females cease relying on other wolves to bring them food and begin to seek their own food. The quickest and most reliable method of getting food is to go directly to an existing kill. After wolves, including yearlings, return and regurgitate food to the pups, mothers will follow their scent trail back to a kill to eat.

The cost/benefit ratio of yearling presence may be directly related to the food supply. During Linda's study food was abundant, and she observed yearlings returning to regurgitate food to pups—but not a lot. In times of less available food, Linda guesses that yearlings might return with even less or no food for pups. Yearlings do seem to seek a position in the pack, and if human concepts were applied, they seek approval. For a yearling to bring back food is "a big deal," says Linda. "Yearlings feel popularity."

On the other hand, yearlings occasionally compete with pups for food. Linda has seen a yearling snatch a piece of regurgitated food destined for a pup before the pup could get it. Deb Guernsey added that yearlings may even try to nurse.

When the pups are three months of age, mother is sleeping further away from the den, seeking a little solitude. Linda remembers that 8M also rarely slept near the den but about a quarter mile away. Pups are demanding. Now is the time that yearlings and two-year olds become valuable as babysitters, and some females and some males are simply better caregivers. Some females appear infatuated with pups. Linda believes that these are the best females in training for future reproduction, either with their birth pack or with another pack. Linda notes that 17F would care for and dote on 9F's pups.

By the time wolves are two, their maturity level begins to change. Two-year-olds contribute to hunting. Their skills have increased and they make effective kills by themselves.

Biologists have hypothesized that if a female spends a lot of time with pups, she will not be as good a hunter. In Linda's experience, it appears that the females who spent more time with pups were better hunters and more active during the hunt. Linda cites 17F, who became alpha of Chief Joseph pack, as a prime example. 17F was an excellent hunter and still infatuated with her own pups.

Wolves are individuals, and personality traits detected in young pups may continue throughout their life. Compare 42F and 105F. Although dominated by her sister, 40F, 42F was aggressive and bold. She excelled as a hunter, being fast, bold, and quick to kill elk even by herself. On the other hand, 105F, 42F's daughter, was always timid. She would travel at the back of the line and lacked aggressiveness when seeking food at kills. These differences were evident after the death of 40F.

Anne Whitbeck, a wolf watcher who seasonally migrates from Colorado to Lamar, was watching the den site south of the river where 42F, 103F, and 105F tended 42F's pups. Anne remembers being the first to spot 42F crossing the river's alluvial fan with something black in her mouth. Shocked, Anne finally comprehended it was a pup. Bold 42F was attempting to move her pups five miles to the old Druid Peak den site, crossing two rivers and a highway in the process.

Anne and others watched as 42F moved one, then a second, then a third pup, and 105F tried to help. 105F took a pup in her mouth and started trotting east. 105F descended into the river bottom, but there were people along the edge of the water. 105F abruptly aborted her travel and returned to the den. 105F had the desire to help but lacked the conviction to see it through. To this day, 105F remains timid in her actions.

PLAY

Play is the tool of education for wolves. Pups that run the fastest, jump the highest, and dominate the most subordinates may be alpha wolves someday. Play teaches wolves!

One day in the summer of 1999 Rick McIntyre watched 21M and some other wolves in Lamar. A young, apparently male pup approached 21M and solicited play. Usually the big, old males, especially alpha males, decline such socialization. But today was different; 21M was in the mood.

As the situation developed, Rick became amazed—21M was playing. The biggest, strongest wolf in the pack was play fighting with his son, *and the pup was winning.* The alpha male was letting a mere pup wrestle him to the ground and stand dominant over him. 21M would get free and regain his standing posture, only to be pinned to the ground again by his son. Then both wolves would do it again. Apparently 21M was so secure in his alpha status that he could allow the young male to win.

Why did 21M let his son win? What was 21M's motivation? Fun? Play? What about something deeper? Play does serve as training and Rick likes to speculate on how 21M might have been training his son. Rick suggests two hypotheses. First, Rick reminds us that "different packs do encounter each other and territorial disputes occur." By "winning" against 21M, the pup learned it had the potential to fight another wolf and defeat it. Second, fighting allowed the young wolf to experience what it felt like to wrestle with a larger animal and to use leverage to bring down that animal, knowledge that would be valuable in hunting. "Wrestling was teaching the young wolf what hunting was all about," Rick said.

Which pup was involved? Rick does not know because pups look alike and are not collared. But Rick likes to think that the son grew to be a prominent wolf in his own right, perhaps the alpha of his own pack and a teacher of pups.

It is apparent that many behaviors we witness and call play actually serve the purpose of training pups. But do wolves ever play just for play? I think so and so does Deb Guernsey. One time Deb was up in a plane scouting for radio-collared wolves. On this particular flight, she had already had spent a long time searching for the Delta pack around the southeast end of Yellowstone Lake. She had radio signals but could see no wolves.

Out of the corner of her eye, Deb glimpsed a wolf streak from the forest onto the lake's frozen ice. She watched, transfixed, as 15 more wolves came charging out of the trees. The ice was slick. Putting on the brakes, the wolves slid into each other. Adults and youngsters burst into a fit of play: sliding, bumping, running, and rolling. None seemed aware there was a plane above with watchful eyes focused on their antics. Play? Most certainly. Learning? Training? Well, maybe.

ECOLOGY

The visibility of wolves in the Yellowstone ecosystem provides a unique window into the intricacies of ecological processes such as competition, predation, and symbiosis.

COMPETITION BETWEEN SPECIES

Coyotes

"In March 2000 I witnessed one of the most intense behavioral sessions I had ever seen. It was bitterly cold and windy. About 30 minutes before sunset, we saw five wolves moving west on top of a hill. They came to a stop and sat down, looking downhill toward us. At first I thought we were attracting their attention, but as I looked down the fall line from the wolves, I discovered three coyotes. Two coyotes were watching the wolves while a third coyote higher on the slope was apparently sleeping.

After several minutes, the wolves started walking directly at us, one at a time. The first wolf was 40F. She would walk a few steps and freeze. After repeating the walk/freeze cycle about three times, she would sit down. Another wolf would move with the same walk/freeze cycle. Occasionally more than one wolf would be moving at the same time, but the overall picture was one of little movement.

The two coyotes eventually became uneasy as the distance narrowed. They moved off and one began to bark, loudly and fairly continuously. The sleeping coyote did not seem to be aware of what was happening, and the wolves were getting closer. Finally the sleeping coyote got up, spotted the wolves, and moved uphill towards them.

We were cold and as it was fast nearing dark, but we were ready for action. After about ten yards, the coyote turned and dropped downhill toward the other coyotes. The coyotes were getting ready to make their escape. Suddenly 40F broke into a full gallop toward the coyotes with 21M only a short distance behind. The chase was on.

The coyotes fled as fast as they could. Two dropped towards us, then cut in front of us with 40F closing the distance. As 40F passed us, she turned and looked at us for a moment. The two coyotes galloped east. The lower one kept looking over its shoulder at its pursuers and ran headlong into a wire fence forming a research exclosure. The coyote bounced on the ground, got up, and shook itself off before hightailing it down to the road for a getaway. The second coyote went high above the exclosure with three wolves in hot pursuit. There was just enough lead that the coyote got away. Sometime during the melee, the third coyote also disappeared. Chase over, the wolves went back up the hill to the rest of the pack. This time they did not get a coyote, but that is not always the case.

In May 1995 Deb Lineweaver and Jason Wilson watched the Crystal Creek pack moving at a steady lope towards a spot southeast from the confluence of Soda Butte Creek and the Lamar River. Wolf watchers were just starting to learn things from the recently released Yellowstone wolves; today would be a big lesson.

Six wolves traveled single file towards a hill. Jason still isn't sure if it were by design or accident, but the wolves approached a pair of coyotes. The coyotes attacked. They charged straight into the wolves but did not make contact. The wolves didn't press the issue. Finally the coyotes got the wolves to chase them a short distance. Then it dawned on Jason and Deb that the coyotes were trying to draw the wolves away from their den.

A Nez Perce wolf explores the Lower Geyser Basin. It has been about seven decades since wolves last roamed in front of White Dome Geyser. The return of wolves has changed Yellowstone's ecology from prey species to plant life. Biologists call the process a "trophic cascade." JESS R. LEE

The interaction went on for a few minutes, but the wolves were not too excited about the coyotes. Most of the wolves laid down about 50 yards from the den, but one wolf started digging in the coyote den. Deb remembers it was a study in contrasts. "The coyotes were going out of their minds. The wolves were so laid back, no frenzy," she recalled. One wolf would dig, come out and shake, and then go back up the hill. Another wolf would go down and dig.

Jason remembers that as each wolf took its turn digging, it would disappear farther from their sight. Finally, the last wolf to dig disappeared completely into the enlarged den hole. "In our minds, the coyote pups had been had," Jason said. The alpha male, 4M, was the last to dig. Then all the wolves wandered off.

Within five minutes after the wolves left, one of the coyote parents was at the hole. Jason and Deb did not see any pups, and the parents disappeared. They knew from Bob Crabtree, coyote biologist, that the coyotes had five pups. Jason and Deb suspected the coyotes would have to try for a family next year.

When all the animals left, Jason and Deb went to the Lamar trailhead to cross the foot bridge and hike to the ravaged den site. Soda Butte Creek was in flood stage and the only reasonable way to the den was over the bridge. As Jason and Deb approached the bridge, the two adult coyotes and two pups a6pproached the bridge from the far side. The coyote parents crossed the bridge but the pups panicked at the sight of it. One ran up into the sagebrush and the other tried to swim. Soon the swimmer was back on shore; it realized that high water is not a place to be.

The adults returned and tried every way to get the pups across. The only solution was to carry the pups. But the nine-week old pups were too big. "The parents tried every way they could to pick up a pup," Jason said. "They put it down on the ground and rolled it over and tried to get a grip, but there was too much loose skin and too big a belly. Then they'd roll the pup around again and try again to grab it." Finally, the parents crossed the bridge and this time the pups followed. Researchers at the

For the coyote, it is a race of life and death. For wolf 42F, it is simply a matter of canid territoriality. Most wolves are quick to dispense of other canid interlopers, but 40F, 42F's sister, developed a well-known reputation among wolf watchers for chasing—and killing—coyotes. 42F eventually caught and killed this coyote. As shown in these photographs, the size difference between a mature wolf and an adult coyote is dramatic. For decades coyotes were the "top dogs" in Yellowstone. Like other park wildlife, they are now adapting to the "new" order. The relationship isn't totally to the coyote's detriment. Wolves are better than coyotes at killing large animals, so coyotes have more carcasses to scavenge. MONTY DEWALD.

trailhead had to stop traffic to let the coyotes lead their pups up the hillside to safety.

When Jason, Deb, Bob Crabtree, and others arrived at the den site, they discovered adult coyote tracks in the fresh dirt at the den entrance. On top of the adult tracks were exiting pup tracks. The pups had been at the bottom of the den. Bob believed the fact that the coyotes moved their pups within 15 minutes after the attack showed their great fear of their new, larger, canine relative.

The next day Jason and Deb again visited the site. It had rained hard during the night, washing out yesterday's tracks but fresh wolf tracks were evident in the mud. The wolves had returned and checked out every den entrance. Clearly, this was no place for a coyote to be, pup or adult.

Later, Dr. Elaine Anderson and I took our wolf class to the coyote den site. Elaine, one of the world's leading Pleistocene paleontologists, stood about five foot tall, and everyone who knew her, loved her. Wolves had widened the den but we still couldn't see to its very end.

Someone had to go in, and Elaine disappeared. Really, her whole body was gone from sight.

Elaine measured the wolf-widened tunnel to be 58 inches deep. Off to the side she found a room with a diameter of 42 inches. Then the coyote tunnel narrowed to 12 to 16 inches. The total length from ground surface to where the tunnel turned beyond Elaine's view was 92 inches. Both coyotes and wolves had moved significant dirt.

We searched the surrounding area and found the mangled carcass of a coyote pup. Apparently all the pups didn't make it. Wolf watchers now call this area Dead Puppy Hill.

Detailed knowledge about relations between coyotes and wolves is provided by Bob Crabtree and Jenny Sheldon and their collaborators. Their exhaustive studies of coyotes date to about seven years before the wolves came to Yellowstone and continue today. Bob and Jenny tell us that coyotes were the top predators on the Northern Range prior to the arrival of wolves. They estimated a population of 400 coyotes and that they killed 1,100 to 1,400 elk per year, mostly calves less than a year old. Coyotes also took a number of sick elk and yearlings. Most instances when coyotes killed healthy adult elk would occur when elk were hindered by snow.

With the arrival of wolves, coyotes turned to scavenging wolf kills. However, since both canids need the same food source, competition does occur. Competition may be either indirect exploitation of a resource or direct interference. Exploitation competition, for example, results from deer, elk, and bison all grazing on grass. Interference competition results from fighting or killing the other species.

Both exploitive and interference competition exists between coyotes and wolves, but interference competition has been the hallmark of the coyote-wolf relationship. Bob and Jenny report that wolves killed 15 coyotes in the 200 encounters they observed from 1996 to 1998. More recently, Bob has said that 50 percent of the coyotes in the core-use areas of the wolf pack have been killed. Some coyote packs have lost one or both alpha animals. The end result is that the number of coyote packs has gone down in Lamar Valley.

Numbers are the key. All observed kills of coyotes have involved three or more wolves on a single coyote. However, when the number of coyotes is greater than the number of wolves, results may favor the coyote. One day we watched as 42F accidentally approached a coyote den housing pups. The adult coyotes attacked and, for a moment, we watchers held our breath as it look like 42F's demise. Luckily other wolves came to her rescue and all wolves quickly left. Twice I have watched as several coyotes drove single wolves away from carcasses.

For coyotes, an elk carcass is too precious to waste. Coyotes are survivors and can lose up to 30 percent of their body weight in a lean winter. But eventually coyotes will risk encounters with wolves to get food. At a kill site, coyotes tend to stand back until wolves have eaten their fill. Then the coyotes try to hit and run, dashing in to grab quick bites or pieces. Non-satiated wolves may give chase, sometimes catching and killing the coyote.

Doug Smith reports a curious interaction among coyotes, a wolf, and a bison. On March 24, 1999, researchers during a flight saw a young wolf, one to three years of age, biting a bison calf by the throat. At the same time, four adult coyotes were biting the bison's hindquarters. Apparently the bites to the throat were fatal. When observed a second time 30 minutes later, the wolf was feeding on the carcass and the coyotes were bedded about 60 yards away. The simultaneous attack is unusual, but even though the coyotes had to wait to eat, it may have been beneficial for both species.

Red fox

For wolf watchers a delightful perk is a three-dog day; that is, sighting wolves, coyotes, and red fox all in one day. The only fox in Yellowstone, the red fox is diminutive, secretive, and a delight to watch. Being at the bottom of the canid hierarchy, these animals seem to prefer the night and the forests, while coyotes prefer twilight and daylight situations. Each winter though, red foxes are seen scurrying across the open flats. I think they venture out into the open when snow conditions are poor in the forest.

Before wolf restoration, biologists speculated that the presence of wolves would allow fox populations to increase. The logic was that coyotes compete with foxes and kill foxes. Bob Furhman, our resident fox expert, says that prior to reintroduction, foxes were found mostly in less frequently used areas at the periphery of coyote territories. Therefore, coyotes kept fox numbers down. Since wolves would reduce coyote numbers, pressure would be reduced on foxes and their numbers would increase.

No one has ever counted Yellowstone's foxes, so information about the effect of wolves is anecdotal. From my experience, during the winter of 1992 fox were the most abundant since I started conducting programs in Lamar Valley in 1972. In the winter of 2000/2001, fox numbers appeared to be up, as there were many sightings. However, the number of sightings was up not only in territories used by wolves but also in areas outside wolf territories. In the winter of 2001/2002, the number of fox sightings decreased.

Claiming an increase in the fox population due to the presence of wolves appears to be premature. There may be additional factors, including snowpack conditions within the forests versus in the open. Observers need to allow a few more years for this scenario to play out completely.

Wolves do prey on fox. In fact, the first animal killed in Yellowstone by the wolves was a red fox. It seems that while the wolves were in their acclimation pen, a fox climbed the wire fence and dropped into the pen to scavenge at a carcass left by biologists. It was a fatal error.

Grizzly bears

The African lion may rule as king of the beasts in the Serengeti, but in North America's Serengeti, the Lamar Valley, the grizzly bear is king. Yellowstone's biggest carnivore, males average about 450 pounds with a record weight of 717 pounds. Few animals, including humans, care to cross an adult grizzly. The prediction is that grizzlies will benefit from the reintroduction of wolves but not necessarily win every conflict.

Grizzlies are fast predators, but only fast enough to run down elk calves during the first month or so of the calf's life. After elk calves are 60 days old, grizzly predation diminishes dramatically. Then the grizzly's best strategy is to take advantage of wolf predation.

Grizzlies may take prey during wolf predation events or take over a carcass after a wolf kill. One time Dan MacNulty and Nathan Varley witnessed an interesting act of dual predation. The encounter was between five adult wolves from the Crystal Creek pack and a single grizzly. On March 23, 2000, the grizzly had closely followed the wolves on three occasions as they tried unsuccessfully to attack a herd of 59 buffalo.

On the 24th, the standoff continued but only nine bull bison and an 11-month-old calf were still involved. Wolves managed to inflict visible damage to the calf during the earlier part of the day, but the bulls kept the wolves at bay. Finally seven bulls walked away. The remaining bulls and calf started to leave, but deep snow hindered the calf and it dropped back 10 to 15 yards.

Sensing vulnerability, wolves approached from the west but the grizzly came in from the east. Wolves ran past the bulls and grabbed the calf. Three wolves let go to charge the grizzly. The grizzly feinted retreat and then charged past the wolves to attack the calf's hind end with its forepaws. Three wolves bit the front end of the calf at the same time. The grizzly pulled the calf from the wolves and began to feed. The wolves eventually lay down within five yards of the grizzly as it fed. Then the nine bison bulls returned and spooked the grizzly off the carcass. The wolves immediately possessed it and began to feed. Nineteen minutes later the grizzly returned and displaced the wolves to feed again.

The situation reflects the complexity of predator-prey interactions. In general, grizzlies tend to usurp carcasses from wolves simply because of their size. For wolves, the wisest strategy is to wait to feed. Dan suggests that "kleptoparasitism by grizzly bears...could be a factor favoring the evolution of group living in gray wolves."

It is interesting to note that grizzlies seem to know that wolves may lead to food. In the fall of 2002 Wayne Kendall watched 106F's

pack pass his observation point. About 30 minutes later, a grizzly followed along their trail, tracking the wolves by their odor for about two miles.

Researchers are closely watching the wolf-grizzly interactions in Yellowstone for another phenomena: cessation of bear hibernation. In Glacier National Park, it appears that some grizzlies may avoid hibernation by feeding on carcasses provided by the increasing wolf population. Time will tell.

Not all interactions end in favor of grizzlies. In the summer of 1995 I watched as a grizzly killed an elk calf and dragged it into a small clump of trees on a hillside. Harassing wolves charged into the clump only to run out again moments later. Then 4M, alpha male of Crystal Creek pack, galloped down the hillside from above the trees and entered the clump going full bore. Nothing happened for a few seconds. Then 4M broke from the bottom edge of the trees carrying a front quarter of the elk. He kept on going as the grizzly broke into the open after him, but 4M had too much of a head start.

The outcome of a particular interaction over a carcass may depend on several factors, including degree of satiation, number of hungry young, and number of each species. Wolves or grizzlies with full stomachs will often give up a carcass easily. However, mothers with young tend to be more possessive. Many wolves may displace a grizzly when one or two would not.

While few creatures will fight an adult grizzly, cubs are vulnerable. In fact, a species can be driven to extinction without adult mortality

In a tense moment, Crystal Creek wolves challenge a grizzly bear for a carcass in Pelican Valley. The winner of the carcass was probably determined by motivation. Hungry wolves may drive a grizzly from a kill, but a grizzly can usually take over a carcass from wolves, especially if the wolves have already fed. The relationship between wolves and grizzly bears is complex. Wolves may attack and kill grizzly cubs, but grizzlies gain a food source by scavenging wolf kills. DOUGLAS SMITH/NPS

if enough young are killed. And wolves do kill young grizzlies. Observations in Lamar Valley seem to indicate that the Druid Peak pack killed a grizzly cub-of-the-year (COY) in both 2001 and 2002.

Wayne Kendall related this story of cub killings in 2002. Wolf watchers had been entertained for several days by a sow grizzly and her two COYs as they fed along the bottom of Lamar Valley. On Saturday night, May 18, she was last seen with her two cubs near the Druid Peak den. On Sunday morning, watchers saw a sow with only one cub. Most thought it was the same sow but she had probably lost a cub to the wolves.

On May 22, the sow and COY came off a hillside to the north and headed for a day-old carcass south of Lamar River. She either smelled the carcass or already knew its location because she bee-lined for it. Wayne was watching three wolves feeding on the carcass. He thinks the bear didn't know the wolves were there, for he believes she would not knowingly have brought her cub into such a dangerous environment.

In the middle of the flats, the wolves noticed the bears and dashed at them. Whether the wolves were intent on keeping her away from the carcass or making a meal of the cub could not be ascertained. The sow noticed the wolves as they closed to 50 yards and immediately used a forepaw to scoop up her cub and place it under her body. The wolves surrounded her at a distance of five to 10 feet.

The wolves took turns moving in to nip at the sow in an obvious attempt to get her to chase them. The sow would not take the bait, only swatting and biting at the wolves. She stood her ground, frequently checking to make sure the cub was under her. The wolves tried a new tactic: two charging in at the same time but from different sides. The sow would whirl and slash at the wolves with her front feet, then check for the cub. This went on for 20 minutes, followed by a staredown lasting an hour.

A grizzly mother successfully protects her cub from a wolf attack. During the attack the bear stood over her cub, seldom moving more than a few feet to lunge or swipe at the attacking wolves. She would quickly cover her cub again, sometimes using a paw to tuck the cub close to her body. The cub's head is visible just below the mother's head. It is believed this grizzly had two cubs but lost one of them to the same wolves a few days earlier. Two cubs would be more difficult to protect during a circling attack by several wolves. WAYNE KENDALL

Eventually two wolves were left, one remaining five feet from the bear. Sensing the change, the sow stood on her hind legs to look for the other wolves. Then she started nursing her cub. Our sow then became aggressive, chasing the closest wolf, then standing and looking to make sure she was not being lured away. Finally the wolves left, and the sow and cub trotted off the way they had come.

This behavioral interaction suggests interesting questions. Had the sow learned, through the loss of her other cub, how to stand over her cub to protect it from attack? Had she lost the other cub because it was not possible to keep two cubs under her at the same time? We will never know, but the circumstantial evidence is strong that wolves have been successful predators on grizzly cubs.

The total number of wolves is critical to any interaction. In the fall of 2001, Druid Peak pack had 37 members. On several occasions we observed this superpack, as it was called, harass adult grizzlies. One time I watched 22 wolves strung out in a single file pursuing a grizzly up a hill. Another time approximately 30 wolves surrounded a grizzly. With all these wolves surrounding and biting at a grizzly, the grizzly is likely to sustain injury. As yet, no adult grizzlies have been killed by wolves.

Not all encounters between grizzlies and wolves are aggressive. At 8 a.m. on June 11, 1997, Wayne Kendall watched a sow grizzly and two COY wander along Slough Creek. Just as they entered a slight depression with a small aspen stand, Wayne noticed 53, a black, yearling wolf believed to be a female, following the bears.

The bears noticed the wolf and stopped, whereupon the wolf came within 15 yards of the mother bear. Anticipating a charge, Wayne waited breathlessly with his video camera rolling. But the bear sat down and began to nurse her cubs. The wolf circled and came as close as five feet. For the next eight hours, all four animals stayed within a hundred yards of each other.

Several bouts of playful chasing took place. The COYs would chase the wolf as it would playfully run ahead of them. After each chase ended, the wolf would return even closer to the cubs, at one point coming virtually nose-to-nose. None of the animals ever made an aggressive move, including the sow.

The sow would allow the wolf to approach as long as she was nearby. However, if while chasing the wolf, the cubs ventured more than 30 yards from mom, she would charge ahead of them. There she would position herself broadside between the wolf and cubs, signaling game over. Then she would return to her resting spot, cubs in tow.

Games were repeated throughout the day, only to be interrupted by nursing and naps. When the sow nursed, the wolf would come within several yards, lay down and watch, head resting on forepaws. When the bears napped, the wolf would nap about 50 yards away.

Wayne believes the entire interaction was one of curiosity. At no point did he observe any aggressive activities. The wolf had many opportunities to grab a cub but never did. The sow did not seem to care how close the wolf got, but when her cubs chased it off a ways, it was like an alarm and she went after the cubs, not the wolf.

The sow never made an aggressive attempt to end the play until 4:15 p.m. When the bears and wolf awoke from a nap, the wolf approached. The sow made a small charge at the wolf and swatted at it with a paw. Apparently playtime was over. The wolf ambled off in one direction, the bears in another.

Cougars

The other consummate predator of North America's Serengeti is a lion, known as mountain lion, cougar, puma, catamount, and more than 200 other names. Cougars and wolves are the only predators that kill a substantial number of adult elk. As such, they are in direct competition for food. Cougars prefer open forests more than

wolves do, and wolves prefer open meadows. Still, interference competition is inevitable.

Kerry Murphy, Toni Ruth, and their field crews are seasoned veterans of the physically hardest predator study in Yellowstone: the cougar project through the Hornocker Wildlife Institute. To do what Kerry named a "predator sequence," they will stay on the trail of a cougar for days at a time, tracking the cougar from one kill to the next. Through their efforts we have gleaned some knowledge about the rare, hidden interactions between wolves and cougars.

About 70 percent of cougar kills are elk and about 17 percent are mule deer, compared to wolves that take very few mule deer. Cougars appear to take proportionally more calves and cow elk than wolves do, while wolves take proportionally more bulls. Cougars, like wolves, take malnourished or weaker elk, especially when preying on adult elk.

Toni explains that wolves sometimes displace cougars from their kills. These instances may involve female cougars with kittens. Tony tells of a female cougar trying to feed her young at a lion-killed carcass. In two attacks, the wolves killed all four kittens. Kittens and adults may escape wolves by climbing trees.

The net result of cougars being quickly displaced from their kills is that they may have to kill more frequently. Hunting is replete with dangers, so more hunting may increase cougar mortality over the long run.

Sometimes the situation may be reversed. For example, one March morning I neared the Hellroaring Overlook and spotted cougar tracks in the thin layer of snow on the road. There were lots of tracks, some big, many small. I pulled into the parking lot to find Tom Zieber waving to me to come quickly. Tom has volunteered for several years with the wolf project and specializes in wolf behavior. Tom directed me to a spotting scope. There in the field of view were three cougars: a female and her cubs feeding on an elk carcass.

Tom explained that he had discovered the kill the day before but there were no animals on it. As he watched, several wolves approached. The lead wolf sniffed and jumped back, startled. The wolves then cautiously walked around the carcass and left the scene. When Tom arrived at daylight, the cougars were on the carcass. Tom figures the wolves smelled fresh cougar and were uneasy with the situation, so they skipped a free meal.

Maybe avoiding a free meal in some circumstances is wise. A location that allows a cougar to hide in cover could be fatal for a wolf. Val Asher, biologist for Turner Endangered Species Fund, discovered an apparent cougar predation on a wolf. While following up on a radio collar signal that indicated a possible wolf death, she spotted tracks of a galloping wolf. Backtracking, Val discovered a blood spot, an initial attack site. Continuing along the trail, she found wolf hair clinging to some brambles and a fence. Further radio tracking revealed the radio signal beneath a pine tree. There, underneath about six inches of pine needles, Val discovered the carcass of 297F. Scouting the scene Val found large and small cougar tracks, possibly indicative of a female lion with at least one cub.

Evidently a mother cougar chased down one of two wolves and killed it with a throat bite. Wolves 0, lions 1.

SYMBIOSIS WITH RAVENS

The process by which organisms live and interact together without directly harming each other is known as symbiosis. Ecologists recognize three types of symbiosis: commensalism (one species benefits), mutualism (both species benefit), and parasitism (one species benefits, the other species suffers). The relationship of wolves with ravens is a unique case of symbiosis, one that has elements of all three types.

Researcher Dan Stahler has examined wolf-raven symbiosis in great detail in Yellowstone. Dan explains that it does not take long when observing ravens and wolves to see that something special is happening. Ravens interact differently with wolves than they do with other creatures, including foxes and coyotes. Those interactions suggest a level of knowledge and tolerance between species from which both derive benefit.

Ravens appear to preferentially associate with wolves. In situations where a carcass is not present, Dan observed ravens with wolves 84 percent of the time but with coyotes only 3 percent of the time. Dan also found that ravens were present in more than 80 percent of wolf chases leading to a kill, and if not present, ravens arrived within four minutes after the kill. This suggests that ravens can differentiate between coyotes and wolves and that ravens select wolves because of their greater ability to kill large animals and thus provide food for

Where there are wolves, there are ravens. In Yellowstone, researchers are studying the symbiotic relationship between these species. Ravens benefit from scavenging food at wolf kills, but wolves appear to derive some benefits from ravens too. In one instance, wolves appeared to follow ravens to a carcass the ravens had discovered.
TOM MURPHY

scavenging. Dan noted that ravens do not follow elk, evidently realizing that wolves are a necessary ingredient in the process of turning an elk into a raven meal.

It is possible the association is changing an old ecological balance of the Northern Range. Terry McEnaney, the park ornithologist, suggests that in the past the population of ravens on the Northern Range may have numbered about 120. However, in late winter Dan has observed as many as 135 ravens at one carcass in the Lamar Valley. The high number may represent a seasonal shift of ravens from other parts of the ecosystem.

Sometimes ravens are parasites on wolves, exploiting wolves for the wolves' ability to kill. Soon after wolves make an early morning howl before hunting, ravens appear and follow the wolves. At kills, ravens readily steal meat from carcasses. Dan roughly estimates that a single raven takes as much as two pounds per day. Ravens don't eat all that meat but take some of it to cache for later. With an average of 28 ravens per kill, that is a substantial loss of meat and direct competition for the foraging wolves.

At den sites, ravens occasionally steal from pups, especially young pups less than five weeks old. Theft is accomplished when adult wolves return from a hunt and regurgitate food. During this excitement, ravens steal from inexperienced pups. Dan speculates that some ravens even follow wolves from a carcass back to the den in anticipation of regurgitation.

Sometimes the relationship is commensal with one or the other species benefiting. For example, ravens eat and remove scat from den sites. Although most of the scat consists of inedible bones and hair, some portions of the wolves' diet pass through undigested. Ravens pick through adult scat but swallow pup scat whole. Some scat are cached.

Another commensal relationship facilitates ravens scavenging new carcasses. When ravens, the carcass specialists, discover a new carcass, they approach it with great caution. Often they retreat without even trying to feed. Ravens undergo what scientists call neophobia, or fear of new things. Whereas if ravens observe wolves kill an animal, feeding is nearly instantaneous. Wolves serve as a primary stimulus to feed. If wolves scavenge a carcass, ravens will sometimes start feeding on it also.

Mutualistic benefits are also apparent. Dan reports incidents relayed to him by Rick McIntyre in which raven activity caused wolves to change direction and come to carcasses the ravens had located. On December 16, 1999, Rick observed about 35 ravens flying over Druid Peak pack as it traveled along the valley floor. Soon the ravens flew about a quarter mile away and landed on the snow. Two minutes later the wolf pack turned and traveled through deep snow

Hungry coyotes approach 21M as he feeds on the remains of an elk just downstream from the confluence of Soda Butte Creek and Lamar River. Coyotes and ravens are prominent scavengers at wolf kills.
CHRISTOPHER BLY

to the ravens. There the wolves uncovered a buried elk carcass. Besides following ravens in flight, wolves may spot raven activity at a carcass because ravens repeatedly fly up and down around the carcass as they change positions and search for edible pieces.

Circumstantial evidence suggests that ravens may locate live elk and attract the attention of wolves to the elk. Ravens have been observed harassing sick and wounded elk. Their mobbing behavior could attract wolves. However, unequivocal proof of this behavior has not been documented. Raven scouting behavior may be mutualistic in that ravens benefit. In the case of a live elk, ravens may get a new food source. In the case of a carcass, the powerful teeth of the wolf may be the key. Elk skin is usually too strong for ravens to break through. Ravens may need wolves to open a carcass for feeding.

The complexity of an interspecies relationship that includes parasitism, commensalism, and mutualism cannot have developed in just eight years since wolf reintroduction. Indeed, a gap of 70 years did not diminish this complicated relationship that must have developed over evolutionary time.

Dan believes familiarity is the key to fine-tuning the symbiosis. Wolves and ravens are with each other 55 percent of the time at the den, 34 percent of the time during the winter when no kill is present, and 98 percent of the time when a kill is present. From the time a pup crawls out of the den, there may not be a day in its life when the wolf does not associate with a raven. During its life, a wolf will interact with other species, but not as frequently or as closely as with ravens.

For the raven, the association reeks of potential danger: one snap of wolf jaws and it is all over. Ravens need to gauge the behavioral intent of the wolves they feed near. A learning process must be involved.

On May 5, 1997, Dan watched the Rose Creek den from afar. The pups were less than four weeks old. The den area was, as usual, the center of attraction for ravens. While the pups were down in the den, ravens would walk to the den entrance and peer inside. Ravens were constantly on the roam pecking at scats, bones, and stealing any bit of nourishment they could find. Two adult ravens would occasionally fly back to their nest with wolf scat. Some recently fledged ravens (recognizable by the pink interior of their mouths and juvenile feathers) walked inquisitively around the den area. Mostly the ravens were waiting for any action, a pup to pop out of a den or an adult to return with food. Raven behavior is food motivated.

Finally eight pups came out as six ravens watched. Two ravens started following the pups, staying about a foot behind them. At this time the pups were still smaller than the ravens. One raven approached and grabbed a pup's tail, gently pulling on it. The pup eventually got away by spinning, and the raven repeated its actions twice more. Then an adult, 18F, jumped up and flushed the raven.

Ravens, skilled and powerful scavengers that they are, could potentially harm or kill young pups. Yet this raven gently tugged the tail, testing what the pup would do. Dan wonders if such interactions might be to familiarize pups with ravens and to teach pups that ravens will not harm them. Such learning might also predispose pups to partially tolerate ravens at carcasses when older.

Ravens must learn how close they can safely get to a wolf and how fast a wolf moves. This process starts when the pups are five to six weeks of age. Then the pups switch from being the chasee to the chaser. As ravens approach, pups stalk them and try to pounce on them

Ravens flush from an elk carcass as galloping wolves arrive. First to the scene is 106F, followed by an unidentified gray wolf, either 163M or 107F. Ravens are found with wolves most of the time, whether at dens, rendezvous sites, hunting trips, or kills. Yellowstone's raven population may be increasing as more food is made available by wolf predation.
DAN HARTMAN

For ravens, learning to be in the proximity of wolves continues with adult wolves, Dan believes. He has observed ravens harassing adult wolves. When wolves are bedded, ravens will pull their tails or peck at their hind feet. The usual result is that the wolf will move away and re-bed. Perhaps harassment of adult wolves allows the raven to learn to interpret the behavioral intent of a wolf.

Averaging 2.4 pounds, ravens are a large portion of potentially available food. But do wolves ever really kill ravens? Scant evidence leaves the impression that wolves seldom kill ravens. While in the acclimation pens during reintroduction, wolves apparently killed one raven. In captive facilities, wolves have been documented killing ravens but only rarely. No one has ever reported seeing a wolf kill a raven in the wild.

The lack of killing and, especially, eating of ravens may reflect the closeness of the relationship between the two species. Bernd Heinrich, leading expert on ravens and author of *Mind of the Raven*, has hypothesized about another possibility: perhaps wolves do not eat ravens because ravens taste bad. Dan did observe a yearling wolf return to the den carrying a raven, but he could not ascertain if the wolf had killed it. The yearling dropped the raven at the feet of pups, who promptly tore it to pieces and ate part of it. Two adults also participated in the meal. Bernd suggests additional tests for edibility.

Dan wonders if ravens might in some way be part of the pack. Both species are social and capable of forming bonds lasting extended periods of time. Both species can recognize individuals. Could some level of cross-species bonding occur? Does one wolf or one raven know or recognize the other? Might ravens be generic members of the pack? A social bond between these species might not necessarily be beneficial to both all the time. After all, it would be symbiosis.

THE TROPHIC CASCADE

For the future, the greatest questions resulting from wolf restoration pertain to the shifting balance of the trophic structure of the ecosystem. Wolves have been described as a keystone species, a species so important to the ecosystem that its removal would affect the ecological pyramid on each trophic level, from plants to herbivores to other carnivores. Therefore, the reintroduction of wolves into an ecosystem should have profound effects that reverberate down the ecological pyramid, a "trophic cascade." When wolves allow changed patterns within the ecological community, it is called a release.

Scavenger release

With the arrival of wolves, food availability for scavengers changed. Dan Stahler, reporting on some of his work with Toni Ruth, says there is a "stark difference" in how cougars affect the scavenger community compared to wolves. Both wolf and cougar kill elk, but scavengers benefit more from a wolf kill because of where wolves kill and how they behave around a kill. Wolves tend to kill in the open, where scavengers can find the carcass. Scavengers feed with an open field of view, so other predators may not sneak up on them. Wolves eat until full and then move off to bed and rest. This allows scavengers a chance to feed.

Cougars kill in more protected and wooded locations, making it more difficult for scavengers to find the cougar's kill. Cougars cache what they don't eat to save for another meal. To cache the meat, cougars take the carcass to a secluded spot and cover it with grass, branches, and dirt. Then cougars bed near the carcass to protect it. Cougars may feed on the same carcass up to a week or until the meat is all gone.

Increased cougar vigilance prevents other scavengers from sharing the carcass. Cougars can and will attack birds coming to their carcass.

Near Swan Lake, a wolf hunts through a marsh. Always looking for an extra meal, the wolf might find the nest of a marsh bird. The effects of wolves on the Yellowstone ecosystem extend far beyond the major prey species of elk and bison. JESS R. LEE

A young wolf, probably from Leopold pack, stands silhouetted against conifers near Phantom Lake. DR. JIM MCGRAW

While ravens may be safe with wolves, that safety margin is slim with a cougar.

Wolves may make previously guarded cougar carcasses available to the scavenging community by displacing cougars. Dan points out that displacement may not be a scavenging effort by the wolves but simply competitive interaction with another predator. Displacing cougars is not without risk, as cougars do kill wolves.

Dan and Chris Wilmers believe wolf kills are more available not only in space but also in time. Wolves provide carcasses all year. Grizzlies are taking advantage of autumn carcasses. During the fall of 2002, grizzlies followed the Druid Peak pack well into December, often immediately usurping the wolf kills. Biologists are closely watching the fall scavenging by grizzlies to see if it will affect their

winter sleep pattern. If food is available, bears may not go into dens for the winter.

Prey release

Flowing down the cascade, the reintroduction of wolves may benefit mammalian prey species such as pronghorn antelope. Doug Smith and John Byers postulate that since wolves are successfully keeping coyote densities lower in the center of their territories, and since wolves take fewer pronghorn fawns than coyotes do, the pronghorn populations should increase.

Pronghorn fawn survival is near nil south and west of Gardiner on the sagebrush/grassland flats of the northern park. Here coyotes kill many if not most fawns. On the Blacktail Plateau, fawn survival is higher, and in the Lamar Valley in the heart of the Druid Peak pack territory, fawn survival is higher still. The anecdotal data supports the prey release theory, and it will be interesting to test this theory over time.

A landscape of fear

Melodramatic but visually indicative, John Laundre calls the relationship between wolves and their prey the "landscape of fear." John, a behaviorist, Lucina Hernandez, and Kelly Altendorf have closely followed elk and bison since the reintroduction of wolves. Their ideas suggest new, even controversial, ways of looking at the effect of wolves on the ecosystem.

John and his team observed elk and bison for five years to see how many times they lifted their heads to scan for possible attack by wolves. Observations were made in areas with wolves and in areas of the park where wolves had not yet arrived.

In areas with wolves, increased vigilance did occur, but contrary to predictions, it did not decrease as herds got larger. Theory holds that with more animals in a herd, each animal can be less vigilant and spend more time feeding. Evidently it is important for each animal to be aware of its surroundings.

Neither bull elk nor bull bison increased their vigilance. John suggests that "reproductive success in males depends on maintaining a maximum body weight." To win the mating battles bulls cannot afford to have low nutritional status or be small; therefore they must continue feeding.

With elk, cows with calves were the first to respond when wolves entered elk range. Cows with calves increased their vigilance about 25 percent, but after two years the increases leveled off. Cows without calves also increased vigilance, but only slightly. For cows, lower

nutritional status does not negate breeding; small cows get to breed also. Therefore, cows can allocate time to vigilance. Females with calves must assure future reproductive chances along with protecting the current investment in their young, so they must be more vigilant.

John's study suggests that increased vigilance reduces the time available for feeding to about half of all non-bedded time. There are many important implications to these observations that warrant additional study. For example, less foraging may result in smaller females, smaller calves and fawns, less milk, and lower survival rates for cows and calves. As a winter ecologist, it strikes me that even the loss of a few calories during summer may critically affect nutritional balance and survival in winter, especially a severe winter. Potential mechanisms to compensate for low nutritional status include longer periods of feeding, shifting feeding time, and shifting locations on the landscape. Shifting locations on the landscape potentially affects other components of the ecological pyramid.

Plant release

Aspen we see today on the Northern Range are but a small remnant of their former majesty. Aspen numbers have decreased dramatically during the last century. Certainly the decline is due, in part, to the fact that elk eat aspen, especially during harsh winters. New aspen suckers (young, tender shoots) stand little chance of survival under the intense browsing of large elk populations. Might not the presence of wolves influence aspen growth?

Bill Ripple, Eric Larsen, Roy Renkin, and Doug Smith believe the effects of wolves have cascaded down to aspen. Their study shows that in low-wolf-use areas, elk foraged twice as much in moist grasslands, stream areas, and wet meadows compared to high-wolf-use areas. In the high-wolf-use areas, sucker heights were significantly taller in stream areas and wet meadows than in low-wolf-use areas. No difference in heights was observed in moist grasslands.

The long term effect on aspen is unclear. From 1923 to 1968, when park elk numbers were controlled and kept low, aspen failed to regenerate into large trees. Apparently even low numbers of elk may suppress aspen growth. Perhaps the Landscape of Fear will provide some areas where aspen will again develop into forests, yet in other areas, aspen may be perennial shrubs, never growing tall.

Aspen aren't the only woody plants being affected by a cascade down from wolves. In the heart of the Druid Peak territory in Lamar Valley, willows are growing higher than I have seen them since 1971 when I first led programs in Lamar Valley. More and bigger willows affect animals from birds to beavers. For example, Doug Smith suggests monitoring the number of Wilson warblers, a willow-loving species, to determine if they are increasing.

The greatest wildlife ecology experiment of the 20th century is showing that wolves can modify the entire Yellowstone ecosystem. Eventually, trophic cascading through behavioral interaction with prey species may affect even the smallest plants. After all, elk tread on small flowers too.

Wolves are changing the landscape of Yellowstone National Park. Some changes, such as the effects on coyotes and ravens, are already visible. Other changes will take more time to unfold. The reintroduction of wolves to Yellowstone has been called the greatest wildlife experiment of the 20th century. Yellowstone may now become the greatest field laboratory for studying and learning about wild wolves.
DONALD M. JONES

WATCHING WOLVES

We can love wolves to death. How can this be? The dilemma is that our presence and our searching for wolves can harm them. From creating vehicle accidents to introducing diseases to habituation-caused removals, our love for wolves can lead to their deaths.

In May 1998 Linda Thurston was watching the den of 9F. Early in the morning, she observed some people near the den, but not too near. Linda's attention was on a wolf kill also near the den. A grizzly came in and took the kill from the wolves. The wolves were harassing the grizzly. As wolves came near, the grizzly would swing at them but never connected. Also watching the grizzly was 9F.

About 5 p.m. 9F started moving pups to a new den site. 9F would grab a pup by the nape of the neck and be gone for about two minutes. Then she'd run back for another pup. Each time she passed within 200 yards of the grizzly and the harassing wolves. All actors in the play ignored each other. Linda stayed until dark, trying to get a complete count of the pups.

Why did 9F chose to move her pups at that time, especially along a route that took her near a grizzly? Had it been the close proximity of the people that morning? We will never know. But it is imperative to realize that our presence, even on the road, may influence wolves that are hypersensitive to their surroundings and what happens there.

It is with this realization that I explain, with hesitation, how to find and see Yellowstone's wolves. Perhaps one day our paths will cross in Yellowstone for I truly enjoy meeting wolf watchers, especially those who know *how* to watch. When we meet, let me know you've been a respectful and educated watcher.

HOW TO SEE YELLOWSTONE'S WOLVES

While the wolves of Yellowstone have been exceptionally visible since their introduction, there are never any guarantees you can see them. However, there are tricks-of-the-trade that biologists and dedicated wolf watchers use that will improve your chances. Most importantly, you have to be in the area when wolves are moving. Wolves may move any time they become hungry, but they tend to move in the mornings just before or after daylight and in the evenings before sunset. Sixty to seventy percent of wolf sightings are between sunrise and 8 a.m., and 30 to 40 percent occur in the evening after 6 p.m. If you want to see wolves, be on site by 5:30 to 6 in the morning. Do as wolves do: get up early and nap in the middle of the day.

Use binoculars or spotting scopes to scan the lower tree line in the valleys and the open patches on the hillsides. Look under the trees and as deep into the forest as you can. Watch for movement and black animals. The black wolves are easier to spot than the gray ones.

Listen carefully for wolf howls. Howls are often difficult to hear and many more people see wolves than hear them howl. Most howls people hear will be coyotes. Learn to differentiate. Barking, yipping, and high-pitched howls come from coyotes. Classic wolf howls are low pitched and often called melodious. However, in the fall and even in the winter, wolf pup howls are impossible to tell from coyote howls.

Watch for elk and bison movement. If elk are very alert and watching one area, or if they move quickly from an area, watch that

The sun sets over a group of park visitors watching wolves from the lower slopes of Druid Peak. Morning and night, wolf watchers will be found along park roads. Watching wolves without disturbing them is crucial to the future of Yellowstone's wolves. BOB WESELMANN

area carefully. Also watch for mother elk charging wolves. If you see females trotting forward with their head held high, look for a predator. Look in the direction the elk are looking.

Concentrations of active ravens may signal a carcass and nearby wolves. If you see ravens randomly walking and pecking at the ground, a large food source is not nearby. Flocks of ravens in the air are good clues; watch where they land.

When driving, watch people along the road. If they are intently watching an area, stop and see why. If they are simply visiting, drive on.

The best months are February though April. January is often too cold for most watchers. By February, temperatures are warming and snow provides a backdrop against which wolves stand out. By the end of April the mosaic of snow and bare ground makes it more difficult to see wolves. May and June are the best summer months. By July, when it gets hot and the biting insects come out, the elk move to higher mountains. The wolves follow them. Fall provides the fewest opportunities to see wolves, but as wolf numbers have increased in Lamar Valley, even sightings in the fall have increased.

Wolves have been frequently visible in Lamar Valley. Since 1995, the current owners of the valley—Crystal Creek, Rose Creek, and Druid Peak packs—have thrilled tens of thousands of visitors with live-action dramas. With more wolves in the park, other areas may offer good viewing opportunities. On the Northern Range of Yellowstone, try Lava Creek to Blacktail Deer Plateau, the Hellroaring Overlook, Roosevelt meadows, Little America, and Slough Creek. The open expanses of Swan Lake Flats, Gibbon Meadows, Firehole Drive, and Hayden Valley have also been productive for watchers.

Now for the responsibilities and caveats.

HABITUATION

Wolves experiencing people in a non-negative manner learn to accept people nearby. This is especially true of young and impressionable pups and yearlings, both of which come equipped with more than their share of curiosity. For wolves, it is like their first visit to a bison herd. Wolves learn that the people of Yellowstone harm them no more, and even less, than bison. In fact, our dilemma is that wolf watchers go out of their way to be good citizens by not disturbing wolves. Eventually, wolves approach people, and here the problems start.

Habituation is the process by which animals lose their fear of people. In Yellowstone, habituation may cause encounters where a person may get bitten. Besides habituation in general, there is food conditioning and the bold wolf syndrome.

(Above) Speeding cars pose a particular danger to wolves. This car has stopped to allow Druid Peak wolves the opportunity to safely cross the road.
DAN HARTMAN

(Left) Two young Druid Peak wolves learned they could safely approach signs, garbage cans, restrooms, and even people. It was necessary for the National Park Service to use aversive conditioning to teach these wolves to avoid humans. Habituation to people could lead wolves into dangerous situations, especially if the wolves roamed outside the park.
JESS R. LEE

Animals that receive food, either directly from people or find food that smells of people, are likely to return to get more food. Food conditioning is rampant in Yellowstone coyotes. Each winter, coyotes learn to beg along the road, where they are hit by vehicles. People trying to feed coyotes can get bitten on their fingers. Regretfully, food conditioned coyotes have to be removed from the population, which usually means death for the coyote.

Food conditioned wolves would be a danger not only to people but also to themselves. Seeking food on or close to the road, wolves may be hit by vehicles. A wolf might bite someone trying to feed it. Doug Smith reminds us that the ultimate fate of a habituated wolf may be death. If visitors act carelessly, it may cause a wolf to die.

Food conditioning has already started to happen. Wolf 104M and two pups from the Druid Peak pack have scrounged food at trailhead garbage cans. Wolf 163M not only carried discarded aluminum cans but also played with them. Wolf watchers can help prevent these unintentional incidents by not littering and not filling garbage cans to overflowing. If the garbage can is nearly full, take your garbage with you. If the can is overflowing, go the extra distance and clean it up and take garbage to a better location.

Worse than accidental food rewards is direct feeding. It has already happened. During the 2001/2002 winter, people in a pickup truck were observed throwing food to wolves. Feeding wolves is a breach of ethics beyond comprehension, and we must guard against it. If food is found on the ground, quickly clean it up.

The bold wolf is a habituated wolf that frequently accepts or may seek out the company of people. The bold wolf may even behave as if people are part of its pack. Bold wolves have been documented in Canada's Algonquin Provencial Park. One wolf lay on a carcass directly across from people who were watching it. When the wolf got up, it came at the people as if to exert its turn to feed. Rangers in Algonquin know from bad experience that bold wolves can harm people, and they immediately remove a wolf when it becomes bold.

Could this happen in Yellowstone? Yes. We have already seen the seeds of boldness in some wolves. While many wolves often walk close to people, 163M made forays through watching crowds and

Watching wolves is thrilling and, when done correctly as shown here, safe for the wolves and the watchers. Avoid close encounters and observe wolves from a distance with binoculars and spotting scopes. Use powerful telephoto lenses to take pictures. Of course, never feed or approach wolves. Maintaining human separation keeps wolves wild, a crucial condition for their survival. MARK MILLER

people standing at the Yellowstone Institute. During the 2001/2002 winter, young wolves from the Druid Peak pack followed students at the Yellowstone Institute as they went to and from their cabins.

During the winter of 2001/2002, habituation, food conditioning, and bold wolf behavior led to a new policy in Yellowstone: aversive conditioning for offending wolves. Wolf watcher Jeanne Muellner recalled fearing for the wolves as rangers shot exploding shells near wolves to scare them away from cars and garbage cans at the Lamar River trailhead. Jeanne explained that she was not afraid of the shots but of what could happen to the pups if they did not learn to fear and avoid humans. Jeannie knew that familiarity comes at the cost of death in rural Yellowstone country. Wolves approaching people outside of Yellowstone would quickly be shot.

For the National Park Service, aversive conditioning is a policy of necessity and not one it likes to instigate. However, the decision has been made to use guns, horns, and other means to frighten wolves that have learned to come too close to watchers or garbage. For watchers, hoping to get a glimpse or better yet a photograph, the policy seems excessively harsh. Those of us who love wolves must accept responsibility for our actions and embrace aversive condition as a mechanism by which managers may save the wolves we love.

SAFETY AND VIEWING ETHICS

Your safety in Yellowstone is your responsibility. Protect yourself from people, traffic, and animals such as bison, elk, or bears. Keep your children under control and away from animals.

To observe wolves, park in turnouts when possible, even if it means driving to a parking pullout and walking back to view. Lock your car when leaving. Walk on the side of the road against traffic and watch for traffic. Drivers may be watching wolves and not the road. If a turnout is not available, you may only pull off onto established road shoulders. Pull your vehicle completely off the road. Never obstruct traffic. Be especially careful near curves. When getting out, push car doors quietly but firmly shut. Turn your car motor off, for silence and to prevent others from breathing exhaust

If animals are close, stay near your car! Whenever possible, view animals from your car, as they are not disturbed as much by cars as they are by people. Drive slowly when near animals.

Do not approach any animal. Large animals may quickly cause injury if they feel threatened or disturbed. By approaching or feeding wildlife you may play a part in their eventual removal and destruction. Do not feed, call, or whistle at wildlife. Never cause an animal to move to where it may become endangered, such as onto a road, into a river, or near a cliff. Intentionally disturbing any wildlife is prohibited by park regulations.

Good viewing etiquette requires that you not bother or molest animals. Your presence should not alter an animal's behavior. If animals change their behavior, such as eating or resting, and begin to focus on you, then you have approached too closely. Move away immediately!

Use telephoto lenses to photograph animals. Do not call, whistle, or attempt to "stimulate" action for pictures. Wait for the animal to move. Do not move in front of others taking pictures.

Quiet, quiet, quiet! Our voices, radios, and motors mask the pristine sounds of wilderness and disturb animals. Your voice can be heard by wild animals, sometimes up to two miles away. Talk softly and listen to nature. At viewing sites be especially quiet. Wolves at den sites will be very sensitive to the presence of humans. Respect their silence.

Do not howl because your imitation howl may appear to be competitive to territorial wolves, and it is illegal.

We must "police" our viewing activities. If others are being loud, endangering wildlife or people, politely ask them to stop. One approach to offenders is to share some of your knowledge about wolves and the need not to disturb them. This may make it easier to get others to lower noise levels. Often unknowing people will quickly change their routines when they understand the impact of their behavior. You may report violations of park rules to rangers. Take pictures to document a serious offense.

Sometimes wolves travel on roads because roads make easy—although dangerous—travel routes. Vehicles have killed 12 wolves in and around the park. Visitors should remember that park speed limits are 45 mph or less.
JESS R. LEE

MY LAST HOWL

During the whole process of writing this book, I have searched for the BLTs I'd use to close the final paragraphs. BLTs are big, large thoughts. I searched my mind. I searched the myriad of experiences others have shared with me. There seemed too many experiences and thoughts to summarize in but a few words. Then, talking with Rick McIntyre, I found my closing in his personal philosophy.

Rick reminds us that early in the 20th century park rangers helped kill the last wolves in Yellowstone. These rangers were not "bad guys." They were simply doing a job dictated by the wildlife managers of that era. The prevailing philosophy was that wolves, and other predators for that matter, were "bad" for the ecosystem. Only years later did we, as wildlife managers and wildlife lovers, learn the error of our ways. Rick says it is personally rewarding to be involved in righting this historic wrong.

The payoff has been the high visibility of the wolves. "In 1994," Rick asks, "what would your prediction have been as to the percentage of days each year people would see wolves in Yellowstone? Five percent? Ten? A bold 20 percent?"

In turns out, wolf visibility has been a mind-boggling success. Rick has kept track of wolf sightings since the beginning. As I write these words on November 20, 2002, Rick tells me that for 650 consecutive days, since February 8, 2001, someone has seen a wolf every single day, somewhere in Yellowstone National Park.

If the visibility has been unprecedented, the impact on those watching has been unfathomable, and the biological lessons we have learned, priceless. As Rick says, "It is as if the wolves are repaying us for their return to their native lands."

(Above) While running through sagebrush north of the Lamar road, 163M stopped to survey the scene. His bulging belly indicated he had just fed and was probably carrying food back to younger pack members.
DAN HARTMAN

(Left) A Druid Peak wolf howls to the pack. The melodious tones of a howl stir the imagination of all who hear it.
MARK MILLER

EPILOGUE

THE MAGIC OF WOLVES

June 26, 2002, Canyon Village, Yellowstone National Park

A mother, father, and four daughters awoke at 4 a.m. to the alarm clock they had purchased in a park store the previous day. It was dark, but they were excited. By 4:30, they were driving north to Lamar Valley.

Mother Christine was pessimistic about their chances, but she wanted to give her daughters a chance to see wolves, so she played along. After all, this trip had been several years in planning and the goal was to see wolves.

Christine, a biology major in college and now a businesswoman, recognized the magic that gripped her family, especially Valerie. The 15-year-old volunteered at the Phoenix Zoo and Adobe Wildlife Rehabilitation Center. She helped during the zoo's wolf awareness week, sharing her book learning about wolves by teaching others. Now was the time to learn first hand, in Yellowstone. They'd seen a moose and its calf in Grand Teton National Park. Would Yellowstone deliver this morning?

At Roosevelt Junction, it seemed to happen. Three wolfish shapes with glowing eyes appeared in the headlights. Chaos reigned in the car until Valerie said no, they were coyotes. On they went to Lamar.

The sky began to lighten. A few cars were parked along the side of the road. Christine remembered that "despite the presence of humans, the valley felt wild, it felt big."

Since their reintroduction in 1995 and 1996, wolves have spread throughout Yellowstone. Although most sightings have taken place in Lamar Valley, wild wolves may be seen almost anywhere in the park. This wolf is leaping over a log while hunting along the Firehole River. JESS R. LEE

After the sun rose, they spotted small groups of people on a rise near the road. The family parked and walked up the hillside. Listening to excited, hushed voices they picked up the word "wolf." A watcher, seeing they had no spotting scopes, offered the family a look through his. Christine stepped forward and there, in the scope, were four adult wolves. "It was a heart-stopping moment," Christine said. "The high-powered scope clearly showed the wind ruffling their fur." Then they heard faint howls.

Excitement reigned and they listened as other watchers told stories of recent sightings. A tall ranger, Rick McIntyre, appeared and shared his knowledge about the wolves. There were four adults and three pups from Druid Peak pack. Rick let Valerie handle the radio receiver. Valerie knew what the receiver was because she had taught others about receivers back in Arizona, but this was real!

Then Rick lined everyone up and started counting. His finger stopped when he was pointing at Christine, and he said, "One hundred thousand." Ever since wolf reintroduction in 1995, Rick and other watchers had been counting visitors who had seen wolves. That day, June 26, 2002, the 100,000th visitor saw wolves in Yellowstone.

It is astonishing that 100,000 visitors have been touched by the magic of wolves. Some have been more than touched. There are hundreds of long-term wolf watchers. A few watchers have immortalized (well, almost) wolves on their license plates. Three plates read Wolf 21M, another says Wolf 39. Some watchers have moved permanently to the Yellowstone area simply to be close to the wolves.

Three people are icons of Lamar Valley and make it a better place to share with visitors and the wolves. They are ranger Rick McIntyre, cinematographer Bob Landis, and retiree Cliff Brown. Day in, day out, fair weather or foul, these three are there. All three are touched with the magic.

I remember a magical moment that happened February 11, 1997, at the Yellowstone Institute. My class stood enthralled as we watched members of the Wolf Project process wolves for transfer. The wolves arrived in carrying cages and were taken into the barn, where biologists quickly did their jobs.

We were standing outside in the cold when then Project Director Mike Phillips came over to us. Mike felt the magic and knew the magic the onlookers were feeling. To our amazement, he invited us inside for the next batch of wolves.

We were told to stand at the far end of the room and be quiet. Quiet? The students didn't even breathe. We crowded in and watched, transfixed. The biologists brought in two anesthetized wolves, a pup and a yearling, probably 29M. The wolves were checked, weighed, and collared. Then Mike said we could touch the wolves. One at a time, with reverence, all moved forward to be part of the restoration of wolves to Yellowstone. All were deeply moved.

One person, Maggie Purves, touched the wolves and came back to my side. Then she collapsed against me, her heart racing. Mutual support probably stopped Maggie from going to the floor. We were both moved beyond words. Maggie now comes back nearly every year. Her donations have supported the wolves on a yearly basis, and Maggie has helped place radio collars on 207M and 260F.

In hindsight, the pup that day was probably 70M or 72M, both now part of the Nez Perce pack and one of them probably the alpha. Maggie believes the genes of the pup she touched that day are spread well into the Yellowstone population.

Indeed, wolves are magical.

The next generation of Druid Peak wolves ascends a slope southwest of Trout Lake. The top gray wolf is 217F and the rest are uncollared yearlings and two-year olds. All are returning to a kill they made the night before. Eight more wolves soon followed these. DAN HARTMAN

ABOUT THE AUTHOR

Dr. James Halfpenny, a scientist and educator, owns A Naturalist's World, a company dedicated to providing educational programs, books, slide shows, and videos about ecologically important subjects. Topics include rare mammalian species, tracking, winter and alpine ecology, and special ecosystems: Arctic, mountain, and African. He is author of *A Field Guide to Mammal Tracking in North America, Discovering Yellowstone Wolves: Watcher's Guide, Tracking: Mastering the Basics* (video), *Winter: an Ecological Handbook, Snow Tracking, Scats and Tracks of the Rocky Mountains* and other titles in this series, and numerous scientific and popular articles. He is co-author of the videos *A Celebration of Bears* and *Living Among Ice Bears*, and he wrote a regular column in *BEARS* Magazine. His fields of expertise include carnivore ecology (especially mountain lions, lynx, wolverine, fisher, marten, bears, and wolves), tracking mammals and dinosaurs, and cold environment ecology (winter, polar, alpine). Key research expeditions include the American East Greenland Expeditions, the first Sino-American survey of endangered mammals on the Tibet-Qinghai Plateau of China, and the Tanzanian Mammal and Dinosaur Tracking project.

Since 1961 Jim has taught outdoor education and environmental programs for state, federal, and private organizations. His clients include the Aspen Center for Environmental Sciences, the Audubon Society, Defenders of Wildlife, National Wildlife Federation, The Nature Conservancy, Sierra Club, Smithsonian, Teton Science School, Wilderness Society, Yellowstone Association Institute, various universities and state wildlife agencies, and Rocky Mountain, Grand Teton, Yellowstone, and Glacier national parks. His programs have been written up in *Field and Stream, Sierra,* and *Outside* magazines and many newspapers including the *New York Times.*

Jim is also a past fellow of the Institute of Arctic and Alpine Research (INSTAAR), University of Colorado, where he served as Field Director of the Mountain Research Station (alpine branch of INSTAAR) and Coordinator for the Long-Term Ecological Research program in the alpine. Jim is a Fellow of the Explorer's Club and has led research expeditions in Antarctica, China, Greenland, Kenya, Tanzania, and the United States. He is a Vietnam veteran, is listed in Who's Who of the World, Science, and of the West, and resides in the Greater Yellowstone ecosystem where he spends as much time in the field as is possible, especially on his cross-country skis. Jim may be contacted at:

A Naturalist's World
www.tracknature.com
(406) 848-9458
P.O. Box 989, 206 5th ST W
Gardiner, MT 59030

APPENDIX 1

APPENDIX 2

1995 WOLVES OF YELLOWSTONE

1996 WOLVES OF YELLOWSTONE

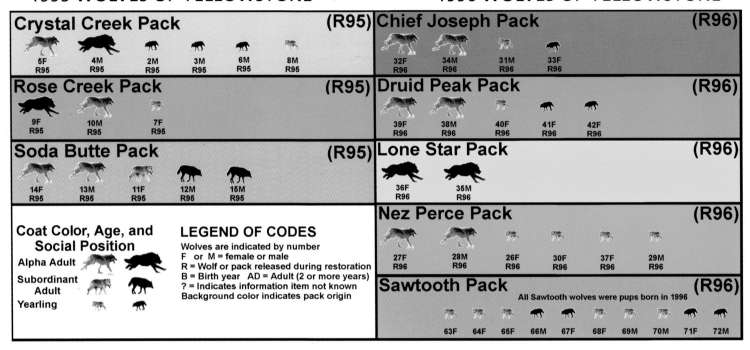

Crystal Creek Pack (R95)

| 5F R95 | 4M R95 | 2M R95 | 3M R95 | 6M R95 | 8M R95 |

Rose Creek Pack (R95)

| 9F R95 | 10M R95 | 7F R95 |

Soda Butte Pack (R95)

| 14F R95 | 13M R95 | 11F R95 | 12M R95 | 15M R95 |

Coat Color, Age, and Social Position

Alpha Adult
Subordinant Adult
Yearling

LEGEND OF CODES

Wolves are indicated by number
F or M = female or male
R = Wolf or pack released during restoration
B = Birth year   AD = Adult (2 or more years)
? = Indicates information item not known
Background color indicates pack origin

Chief Joseph Pack (R96)

| 32F R96 | 34M R96 | 31M R96 | 33F R96 |

Druid Peak Pack (R96)

| 39F R96 | 38M R96 | 40F R96 | 41F R96 | 42F R96 |

Lone Star Pack (R96)

| 36F R96 | 35M R96 |

Nez Perce Pack (R96)

| 27F R96 | 28M R96 | 26F R96 | 30F R96 | 37F R96 | 29M R96 |

Sawtooth Pack All Sawtooth wolves were pups born in 1996 (R96)

| 63F | 64F | 65F | 66M | 67F | 68F | 69M | 70M | 71F | 72M |

SUCCESS AND IDENTIFICATION

The success of the wolf restoration project has been beyond expectations. Reduced knowledge of individual wolves and pack makeup is a key indicator of that success. Each year the wolf chart becomes more complex, but less definite. The percentage of wolves tagged is less, resulting in fewer known wolves. Pack composition becomes more uncertain. Also, greater numbers of wolves mean that wolves often change packs, especially given the close relationships between packs and groups. Wolves often travel between closely related groups every few days. Because of remote locations and difficulties in observing wolves, it is often not possible to definitely know who are the alpha members of the pack. Therefore, consider this wolf chart as a guide to possible identities and packs, but it only represents a snapshot-in-time with changes to be expected whenever new information becomes available, such as additional field research or new DNA analyses as additional wolves are handled.

A BIOLOGICAL AND GENEALOGICAL SNAPSHOT

This annual chart represents a report of the success of the biological wolf year. It is produced at the low point of the population cycle each spring before new pups are born. Therefore, the number of wolves represents those that have survived over the past 12 months. The background color shows genetic relationship. Each pack has a distinctive color and the color stays with dispersing wolves for their life. For example, in the Leopold pack, the alpha female's color shows she came from Rose Creek Pack and the alpha male's origin was Mollie's Pack. The alphas formed a new pack which is colored-coded gray. Therefore, the color genetic trail shows that the alpha female of Cougar Pack is a daughter of Leopold Pack whose grandparents were in Rose and Mollie's Packs. A white back ground means the origin of the wolf is not known.

APPENDIX 3

2002 WOLVES OF YELLOWSTONE

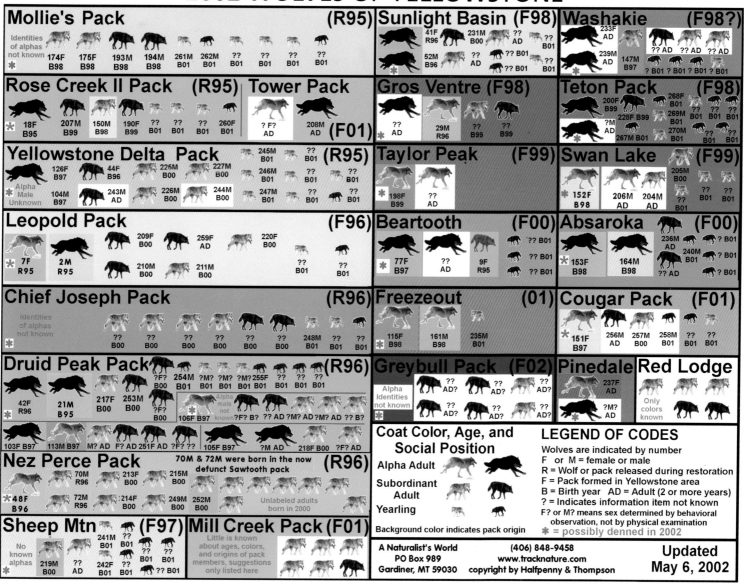

Mollie's Pack (R95)
Identities of alphas not known. 174F B98, 175F B98, 193M B98, 194M B98, 261M B01, 262M B01, ?? B01, ?? B01, ?? B01, ?? B01

Sunlight Basin (F98)
41F R96, 231M B00, ?? AD, ?? B01, 52M B96, ?? AD, ?? B01, ?? B01, ?? B01

Washakie (F98?)
233F AD, 239F AD, 147M B97, ?? AD, ?? AD, ?? AD, ? B01, ? B01, ? B01, ? B01

Rose Creek II Pack (R95)
18F B95, 207M B99, 150M B98, 190F B99, ?? B01, ?? B01, ?? B01, 260F B01

Tower Pack
? F? AD, 208M AD (F01)

Gros Ventre (F98)
?? AD, 29M R96, ?? B99, ?? B99

Teton Pack (F98)
200F B99, 268F B01, ?M AD, 228F B99, 269M B01, ?? B01, ?? B01, ?? B01, 267M B01, 270M B01, ?? B01, ?? B01

Yellowstone Delta Pack (R95)
126F B97, 44F B96, 225M B00, 227M B00, 245M B01, ?? B01, Alpha Male Unknown, 104M B97, 243M AD, 226M B00, 244M B00, 246M B01, ?? B01, ?? B01, 247M B01, ?? B01, ?? B01

Taylor Peak (F99)
198F B99, ?? AD

Swan Lake (F99)
152F B98, 206M AD, 204M AD, ?? B01, ?? B01, 205M B00, ?? B01

Leopold Pack (F96)
7F R95, 2M R95, 209F B00, 259F AD, 220F B00, 210M B00, 211M B00, ?? B01, ?? B01

Beartooth (F00)
77F B97, ?? AD, 9F R95, ?? B01, ?? B01, ?? B01, ?? B01

Absaroka (F00)
153F B98, 164M B98, 236M AD, 240M B01, ?? AD, ? B01, ? B01, ? B01

Chief Joseph Pack (R96)
Identities of alphas not known. ?? B00, ?? B00, ?? B00, ?? B00, ?? B00, ?? B00, 248M B01, ?? B01, ?? B01

Freezeout (01)
115F B98, 161M B98, 235M B01

Cougar Pack (F01)
151F B97, 256M AD, 257M B00, 258M B01, ?? B01, ?? B01

Druid Peak Pack (R96)
?F? B00, 254M B01, ?M? B01, ?M? B01, ?M? B01, 255F B01, ?? B01, ?? B01, ?? B01
42F R96, 21M B95, 217F B00, 253M B00, ?F? B00, 106F B97, Alpha male not known, ?F? B?, ?? AD, ?M? AD, ?M? AD, ?? B?
103F B97, 113M B97, M? AD, F? AD, 251F AD, ?F? ??, 105F B97, ?M AD, 218F B00, ?F? AD

Greybull Pack (F02)
Alpha Identities not known. ?? AD?, ?? AD?, ?? AD?, ?? AD?, ?? AD?, ?? AD?

Pinedale
237F AD, ?M? AD

Red Lodge
Only colors known

Nez Perce Pack (R96)
70M & 72M were born in the now defunct Sawtooth pack
48F B96, 70M R96, 213F B00, 215M B00, 72M R96, 214F B00, 249M B00, 252M B00, Unlabeled adults born in 2000

Sheep Mtn (F97)
No known alphas. 219M B00, ?? AD, 241M B01, ?? B01, 242F B01, ?? B01, ?? AD, ?? B01, ?? B01, ?? B01

Mill Creek Pack (F01)
Little is known about ages, colors, and origins of pack members, suggestions only listed here

Coat Color, Age, and Social Position
Alpha Adult
Subordinant Adult
Yearling
Background color indicates pack origin

LEGEND OF CODES
Wolves are indicated by number
F or M = female or male
R = Wolf or pack released during restoration
F = Pack formed in Yellowstone area
B = Birth year   AD = Adult (2 or more years)
? = Indicates information item not known
F? or M? means sex determined by behavioral observation, not by physical examination
* = possibly denned in 2002

A Naturalist's World
PO Box 989
Gardiner, MT 59030
(406) 848-9458
www.tracknature.com
copyright by Halfpenny & Thompson

Updated May 6, 2002

91

History of 1995 and 1996 wolves

	Wolf	Arr	Death	How	Where
Crystal Creek					
	5F	95	missing	probably deceased	Pelican Valley, YNP
	4M	95	05/21/96	interpack conflict - Druid	Soda Butte Creek, YNP
	6M	95	08/25/98	natural - bull elk	Pelican Valley, YNP
	3M	95	02/05/96	management - sheep	Emigrant, MT
	8M	95	07/??/00	natural - drowning?	Slough Creek, YNP
	2M	95	01/01/03	interpack conflict - Druid?	Blacktail Plateau, YNP
Rose Creek					
	7F	95	05/04/02	interpack conflict - Druid	Blacktail Plateau, YNP
	9F	95	missing	probably deceased	east of YNP
	10M	95	12/19/95	shot illegally	near Red Lodge, MT
Soda Butte					
	11F	95	03/30/96	shot illegally	near Meeteetse, WY
	12M	95	02/11/96	shot illegally	near Daniel, WY
	13M	95	03/19/97	natural - old age	near Heart Lake, YNP
	14F	95	03/??/00	natural - bull moose	near Soda Butte, YNP
	15M	95	10/26/97	management - livestock	Dunoir Valley, WY
Chief Joseph					
	31M	96	12/03/97	shot illegally	Crandall Creek, WY
	32F	96	06/25/96	vehicle	Rt. 191 in YNP
	33F	96	08/08/01	vehicle	Rt. 191 in YNP
	34M	96	11/28/01	natural - bull elk	west boundary, YNP
Druid Peak					
	38M	96	12/03/97	shot illegally	Hoodoo Creek, WY
	39F	96	03/04/98	shot illegally	Sunlight Basin, WY
	40F	96	05/08/00	intrapack conflict - Druid	Lamar Valley, YNP
	41F	96		still present	east of YNP
	42F	96		still present	Lamar Valley, YNP
Lone Star					
	35M	96	02/10/98	interpack conflict - Soda Butte	near Fishing Bridge, YNP
	36F	96	04/14/96	natural - hydrothermal burns	near Lone Star Geyser, YNP
Nez Perce					
	26F	96	06/21/98	management - livestock	Dunoir Valley, WY
	27F	96	10/08/97	management - sheep	south of Dillon, MT
	28M	96	01/27/97	shot illegally	Grey Cliff, MT
	29M	96	missing	probably deceased	radio collar failed 2000
	30F	96	01/09/98	natural - avalanche	near Eagle Pass, YNP
	37F	96	11/26/97	management - livestock	south of Dillon, MT
Sawtooth					
	63F	96	10/26/97	management - livestock	west of YNP
	64F	96	06/06/97	management - sheep	Big Timber, MT
	65F	96	missing	probably deceased	since 1999
	66M	96	07/14/97	vehicle	Canyon to Norris Rd, YNP
	67F	96	08/22/98	management - livestock	west of YNP
	68F	96	09/09/97	management - sheep	upper Green River, WY
	69M	96	07/03/97	management - sheep	near Leadore, ID
	70M	96		still present	west central YNP
	71M	96	05/19/97	management accident-coyote control	south Ruby Reservoir, MT
	72M	96		still present	northeast YNP

Pack and group names and histories

Crystal Creek	restored 1995	renamed Mollie's in 2000
Rose Creek	restored 1995	
Soda Butte Creek	restored 1995	renamed Yellowstone Delta in 2000
Chief Joseph	restored 1996	
Druid Peak	restored 1996	
Lone Star	restored 1996	dissolved 1996
Nez Perce	restored 1996	
Sawtooth	restored 1996	never formed a pack
Leopold	formed 1996	
Sheep mountain	formed 1997	
Thorofare	formed 1997	not located since 1999
Washakie	formed 1998	dissolved 1999
Washakie	reformed 2001	maybe some members from old Washakie Pack
Sunlight Basin	formed 1998	
Jackson Trio	formed 1999	became Gros Ventre 2000
Teton Duo	formed 1999	became Teton 2000
Hellroaring group	formed 2000	Cougar formed 01
Madison group	formed 2000	Taylor Peak formed 2001
Clarks Fork group	formed 2000	Absaroka formed 2000
Sepulcher group	formed 2000	Swan Lake 2000
Gravelly group	formed 2001	Gravelly 2002, relocated outside GYE
Beartooth group	formed 2000	
Mill Creek group	formed 2001	
Freezeout	formed 2002	
Greybull	formed 2002	
Pinedale	formed 2002	
Red Lodge group	formed 2002	

(GYE = Greater Yellowstone Ecosystem)

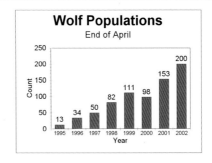

Wolf Populations
End of April

Year	Count
1995	13
1996	34
1997	50
1998	82
1999	111
2000	98
2001	153
2002	200

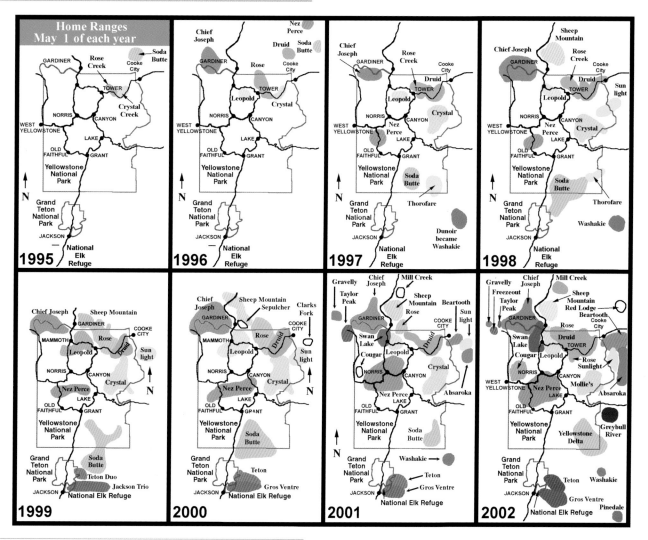

Home Ranges May 1 of each year

1995, 1996, 1997, 1998, 1999, 2000, 2001, 2002

WOLF PACK HOME RANGES

Wolf packs travel long distances looking for prey, learning their home range, and protecting their territory. Ranges are dynamic and boundaries change frequently. Range maps show the approximate area used by each pack during the spring. Shown are core ranges and not exploratory forays made by packs.

All packs have explored outside Yellowstone National Park. Significant since 1997 is the expansion of packs outside the Park. Most areas within the park with wintering populations of elk now have a resident wolf pack.

APPENDIX 8

APPENDIX 9

Growth and Development

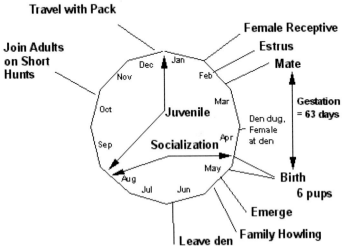

Wolf Year

Travel with Pack

Join Adults on Short Hunts

Female Receptive

Estrus

Mate

Gestation = 63 days

Juvenile

Den dug, Female at den

Socialization

Birth
6 pups

Emerge

Family Howling

Leave den

Jan, Feb, Mar, Apr, May, Jun, Jul, Aug, Sep, Oct, Nov, Dec

AGE	DEVELOPMENT	WEIGHT (lbs)
Birth		<1
11–15 days	Eyes open	4
20 days	Hearing begins	7
21 days	Emergence, play fight	
35 days	Weaning, gallop behind adults	13
8–10 weeks	Abandon den to rendezvous site	15-22
16–26 weeks	Permanent teeth, winter pellage	28-70
27–32	Travel with pack	30-80
52 weeks	Epiphyseal closure	60-100
95 weeks	Sexual maturity	

APPENDIX 10

Weight Distribution
SEX AND AGE

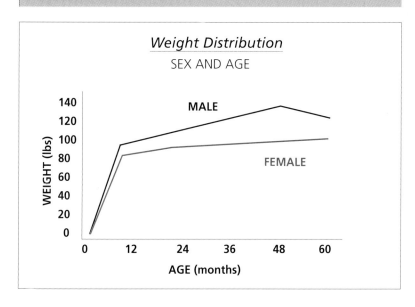

APPENDIX 12

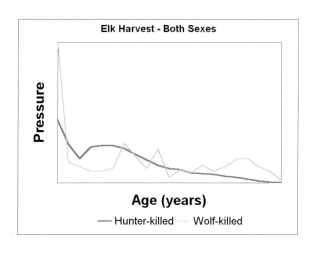

APPENDIX 11

*Largest Yellowstone wolves–
based on weights obtained research handling*

FEMALE	WEIGHT (lbs)*	MALE	WEIGHT (lbs)*
151F	100	012M	122
016F	100	244M	125
030F	100	208M	125
155F	100	122M	125
036F	103	165M	125
014F	104	196M	125
174F	105	193M	128
040F	110	124M	130
042F	110	035M	130
044F	110	204M	130
175F	110	010M	132
126F	111	008M	135
011F	112	055M	135
007F	115	194M	135
027F	115	028M	140
005F	116	006M	141

* Weights may reflect recent meals of 10 pounds or more.

ORGANIZATIONS AND EDUCATIONAL OPPORTUNITIES

Want to be involved? Several organizations provide classes, trips, and support for Yellowstone's wolves. Your interest and participation is welcome.

Park Information

National Park Service
P.O. Box 168
Yellowstone National Park, WY 82190
Phone 307-344-7381
The National Park Service's internet site about wolves:
www.nps.gov/yell/nature/animals/wolf/wolfup.html

Yellowstone Association
P.O. Box 117
Yellowstone National Park, WY 82190
Phone 307-344-2293
www.YellowstoneAssociation.org
The Yellowstone Association is the park's interpretive association and an excellent source for books, maps, and educational opportunities.

Wolf classes and programs in Yellowstone

Yellowstone Association Institute
P.O. Box 117
Yellowstone National Park, WY 82190
Phone 307-344-2294
www.YellowstoneAssociation.org

A Naturalist's World
P.O. Box 989
Gardiner, MT 59030
Phone 406-848-9458
www.tracknature.com

Wolf Recovery Foundation
P.O. Box 44236
Boise, ID 83711-0236
www.forwolves.org

Internet sites about Yellowstone's wolves, including updates of wolf activity

Yellowstone Wolf Tracker
www.wolftracker.com

Ralph Maughan's Wildlife Reports
www.forwolves.org/ralph

The Total Yellowstone Wolf Page
www.yellowstone-natl-park.com/wolf.htm

A Naturalist's World
www.tracknature.com

Wildlife Along the Rockies
www.wildlifealongtherockies.homestead.com

Conversation organizations with specific interest in Yellowstone's wolves

Yellowstone Park Foundation
222 E. Main St., Suite 301
Bozeman, MT 59715
406-586-6303
www.ypf.org
The Yellowstone Foundation's Wolf Fund receives donations and provides financial support for wolf research, including the purchase of radio collars.

Defenders of Wildlife
National Headquarters
1101 14th Street, NW #1400
Washington, D.C. 20005
Phone 202-682-9400
www.defenders.org

Defenders of Wildlife created the Wolf Compensation Fund, a program that provides financial reimbursement to farmers and ranchers who lose livestock to wolf predation.

Greater Yellowstone Coalition
13 S. Willson, Suite 2
P.O. Box 1874
Bozeman, MT 59771
Phone 406-586-1593
www.greateryellowstone.org

Wolf Recovery Foundation
P.O. Box 44236
Boise, ID 83711-0236
www.forwolves.org

National Wildlife Federation
11100 Wildlife Center Drive
Reston, VA 20190-5362
Phone 703-438-6000
www.nwf.org

National wolf education and research organizations

International Wolf Center
1396 Highway 169
Ely, MN 55731-8129
Phone 218-365-4695
www.wolf.org

Wolf Education and Research Center
111 Main Street
Room 150
Lewiston, ID 83501
Phone 208-743-9554
www.wolfcenter.org

An educational, not-for-profit wolf preserve

Grizzly and Wolf Discovery Center
P.O. Box 996
West Yellowstone, MT 59758
Phone 1-800-257-2570
www.grizzlydiscoveryctr.com

RECOMMENDED READING

A Society of Wolves: National Parks and the Battle over the Wolf by Rick McIntyre, 1993 (Voyageur Press)

Birds of Yellowstone by Terry McEneaney, 1988 (Roberts Rinehart)

Discovering Yellowstone Wolves: A Watcher's Guide by James C. Halfpenny and Diann Thompson, 1996 (A Naturalist's World)

Mind of the Raven by Bernd Heinrich, 1999 (HarperCollins Publishers)

The Great American Wolf by B. Hampton, 1997 (Henry Holt and Co.)

The Return of the Wolf to Yellowstone by Thomas McNamee, 1997 (Henry Holt and Co.)

The Way of the Wolf by L. David Mech, 1991 (Voyageur Press)

The Wolf by L. David Mech, 1970 (Natural History Press)

The Wolves of Yellowstone by Michael K. Phillips and Douglas W. Smith, 1996 (Voyageur Press)

The Yellowstone Wolf: A Guide and Sourcebook by Paul Schullery, 1996 (High Plains Publishing)

The Yellowstone Wolves: The First Year by Gary Ferguson, 1996 (Globe Pequot Press)

War Against the Wolf by Rick McIntyre, 1995 (Voyageur Press)

Wolf: Return to Yellowstone by Michael Milstein, 1995 (The Billings Gazette)

Wolf Wars by Hank Fischer, 1995 (Globe Pequot Press)

VIDEO

Wolves: A Legend Returns to Yellowstone by Bob Landis and National Geographic, 2000 (National Geographic)

An example of habituation to people, this young Druid Peak wolf walked from a kill on Crystal Bench down to the road to investigate approximately 20 people who were standing there. He then proceeded to walk onto the road and stood in the middle of it, howling. Later this wolf disappeared. Since it was never radio-collared, its location or fate is unknown. BOB WESELMANN

A NOTE ABOUT THE PHOTOGRAPHS

There are no photographs of captive wolves in this book. That statement may not seem extraordinary, but it is. Most books, calendars, and magazine articles about wolves use all or at least some photographs of captive wolves, even if the wolves look wild. Either the fence is out of the picture or trained animals have been taken to a wild location for a photo shoot. There may be a place for such photographs, but not in a book that celebrates the successful reintroduction of wild wolves into the world's first national park. All the photographs in this book are of wild wolves in Yellowstone.

Some of these images are incredibly beautiful, perfectly composed with perfect light. The photographer was both good and lucky— and dedicated and determined. The best wildlife photographers work harder than most people work. Day after day after day, they look for wolves from before daylight to after sunset. They hope for good light but they can't control it. They pray for wolves to be close but they can't control that either. They must understand wolves, what they do, where they go, and, perhaps most importantly, what they may do next. And they must respect wolves and park regulations. No wildlife photo should mean harassing the subject or breaking the law.

A few photographs in this book are technically poor but illustrate incredible situations. Usually the deficiencies were caused by factors beyond the photographer's control. That's the nature of *wild* life photography.

We think *Yellowstone Wolves in the Wild* is a remarkable book for the new information it presents about wolves and for its all-wild photography. To the photographers who contributed to this book, we say congratulations and thanks.

Riverbend Publishing

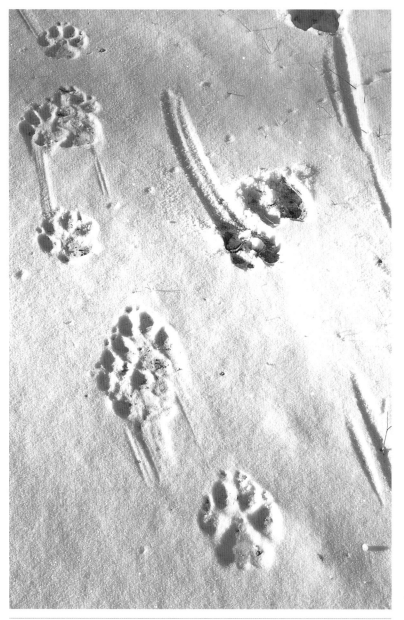

Tracks in the snow emphasize the close link between wolves and elk in Yellowstone.
DONALD M. JONES